Playful Patchwork Projects

Playful Patchwork Projects

Kari Pearson & Friends

Sterling Publishing Co., Inc. New York

A Sterling/Chapelle Book

k.p. kids staff

Kari Pearson: president & designer
Lori Konshuk: director of marketing
Robin Foutch: office manager
Kristin Judd: artist & pattern drafter
Kristi Parry: public relations director & seamstress

Library of Congress Cataloging-in-Publication Data

Pearson, Kari.
    Playful patchwork projects / by Kari Pearson & Friends : K.P.
Kids & Co.
        p.   cm.
    "A Sterling/Chapelle book."
    Includes index.
    ISBN 0-8069-2039-4
    1. Appliqué Patterns.   2. Patchwork. 3. Patchwork quilts.
    4. Quilted goods.   5. Wearable art.   I. K.P. Kids & Co. II.Title.
TT779.P43   1999   99-39262
746.46'041--dc21   CIP

10   9   8   7   6   5   4   3   2   1

First paperback edition published in 2001 by
Sterling Publishing Company, Inc.
387 Park Avenue South, New York, N.Y. 10016
© 1999 by Chapelle Limited
Distributed in Canada by Sterling Publishing
c/o Canadian Manda Group, One Atlantic Avenue, Suite 105
Toronto, Ontario, Canada M6K 3E7
Distributed in Great Britain and Europe by Cassell PLC
Wellington House, 125 Strand, London WC2R 0BB, England
Distributed in Australia by Capricorn Link (Australia) Pty Ltd.
P.O. Box 6651, Baulkham Hills, Business Centre, NSW 2153, Australia
Printed in China
All rights reserved

Sterling ISBN 0-8069-2039-4 Trade
                    0-8069-2123-4 Paper

For Chapelle Limited
Owner: Jo Packham
Editor: Ann Bear

Staff: Marie Barber, Areta Bingham,
Kass Burchett, Rebecca Christensen,
Brenda Doncouse, Dana Durney,
Marilyn Goff, Holly Hollingsworth,
Susan Jorgensen, Barbara Milburn,
Linda Orton, Karmen Quinney,
Leslie Ridenour, Cindy Stoeckl,
Gina Swapp

Photography: Kevin Dilley,
Photographer for Hazen Photography
Photo styling: Brenda Doncouse

If you have any questions or
comments, please contact:
Chapelle, Ltd.
P.O. Box 9252
Ogden, UT 84409

(801) 621-2777
Fax (801) 621-2788
chapelle1@aol.com

Due to the limited amount of
space available, we must print
our patterns at a reduced size in
order to give our patrons the
maximum number of patterns
possible in our publications. We
believe the quality and quantity
of our patterns will compensate
for any inconvenience this may
cause.

Table of Contents

General Instructions

Choosing Fabrics

Choosing fabrics is a personal matter, and we always recommend that you use fabrics that inspire and delight you. We love sewing with bright, happy colors, but we appreciate rich and romantic shades as well. All of the projects shown were designed using 100% cotton, flannel, or wool. We recommend that you prewash fabrics before using, unless otherwise noted. The most important part of choosing fabric is that you have fun doing it. Don't forget to look for our line of brightly colored k.p. kids and co. fabrics in your local quilt shops.

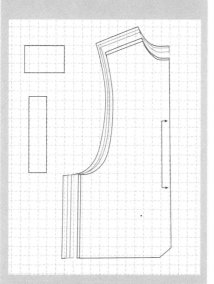

Enlarging Patterns from a Grid

1. Patterns in this book are prepared on a grid in which each square equals 1" on the finished pattern. To enlarge a pattern, select a piece of tracing paper large enough to accommodate the finished size of the pattern. Grid paper is also available at most local craft stores.
2. Mark grid lines 1" apart to fill the paper.
3. Mark dots on the 1" grid lines where the reduced pattern intersects the corresponding grid lines.
4. Connect the dots. Transfer all pattern information, including all markings and instructions.

General Appliqué Instructions

Note: Appliqués are given in one size, but may be enlarged or reduced with a copy machine to fit as you desire.

1. Appliqué Patterns are found on pages 97–126. Appliqué patterns are given in reverse. Using a pen, trace appliqué patterns from book onto tracing paper.

2. Place fusible webbing on top of reversed pattern, paper side up. *Note: All appliqués that are machine-stitched must use lightweight fusible webbing or the webbing will gum up the sewing machine needle.*

3. Cut out pattern on fusible webbing, leaving a ¼" border all around.

4. Using iron, fuse webbing onto selected fabric(s), following manufacturer's instructions.

5. Using fabric scissors, cut appliqués from fabric. If you choose to hand-stitch appliqués onto your project, do not fuse webbing onto them.

6. Remove paper backing and fuse appliqué to clothing or project.

7. Matching thread to fabrics, machine-appliqué around edge with a narrow zigzag stitch.

Tip: On all of our clothing we use tear away backing to stabilize our appliqués. To use, simply place backing on wrong side of clothing directly underneath appliqué. Backing should be at least ½" larger on all sides of appliquéd design. Pin backing in place. After machine-appliqué is complete, tear backing completely away from clothing.

General Embroidery Instructions

1. The following embroidery stitches are used in this book:

    Blanket Stitch

    French Knot (optional for eyes)

    Running Stitch

2. Use 2–6 strands of embroidery floss for blanket stitching, depending on how heavy of an outline or detail you desire.

General Finishing Instructions

1. **Quilting:** Cut backing fabric and batting 2" larger all around quilt top. Pin backing fabric to carpet. Layer batting between quilt top and backing and baste through all three layers. Always start basting your project in the center and work toward the outside. Baste rows about 4" apart. Sew or hand-stitch around shapes, and along borders on quilt. If you would like more stitching on your quilt, then select a design and mark it on your quilt top, using a fabric marker. For more information on quilting, refer to a more instructional book.

2. **Binding:** Cut binding strips 2½" wide on the bias. Sew strips together to form a continuous binding. With WST, fold strips in half lengthwise and press to form a crease. Binding should now be 1¼" wide. Fold one edge under ¼" and press to form a crease. With RST, pin unpressed raw edge of binding to raw edge of quilt top. Sew ¼" seams on front side of quilt, mitering corners as you go. Trim excess fabric and batting even with ¼" seam allowance. Fold binding over edge of quilt. Turn folded edge to back side of quilt and hand-stitch.

General Sewing Instructions

1. Refer to project photos when making project. This will help with fabric choices, appliqué placement, and embellishment ideas.
2. Patterns and templates are included with project instructions.
3. All yardage requirements given are based on 45"-wide fabric.
4. All seam allowances for clothing are ½" unless otherwise indicated. All seam allowances for quilts, pillows, and wall hangings are ¼" unless otherwise indicated.

5. Fabric in diagrams is distinguished by the following:

Right side of fabric

Wrong side of fabric

Lining

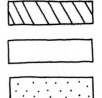

6. Abbreviated sewing terms include RST for "Right Sides Together" and WST for "Wrong Sides Together."

7. Cutting and Preparation instructions contain important information, including sewing steps before actual project construction.

8. You may purchase piping or make your own. To make your own, cut fabric strips on the bias. The width of strips will vary, depending on size of cording you choose. For ⅛" cording, strips should be no less than 1" wide. Sew ends of individual bias strips together for desired length. With WST, fold strip in half lengthwise and finger press. Lay cording inside along folded edge of strip and sew close to cording on the outside, using a zipper foot.

9. The term "seam out" means to make pieces fit uniformly together. To do this, increase seam allowance slightly at the widest area as needed.

Tip: A rotary cutter and mat are helpful for cutting out quilt blocks.

10. A crazy stitch is a freeform quilting stitch. Choose a neutral-colored thread that goes with all fabrics and stitch randomly over project surface.

General Pen-stitching Instructions

1. There are two different pen-stitching techniques. The first is to make small stitches, using a fine-tip permanent black pen, ⅛" from and parallel to edge of shape as shown in Diagram A.

2. The second technique is to make small stitches perpendicular to edge of shape as shown in Diagram B.

Tip: Use an opaque white fabric pen for dark fabrics.

Tip: You can also embroider the details.

Diagram A

Diagram B

Annie & Andy Quilt

Finished size 48" x 60"

The perfect quilt for any toddler, use Annie, Andy, or a combination of the 2 for a quilt that is as colorful as it is fun!

Supplies Needed

Batting:
• 48" x 90"

Fabric:
• for background, 1 yard light-colored
• for backing, ⅔ yard
• for binding, ½ yard
• for checkerboard border, ¼ yard each of light- and dark-colored
• for narrow border, ¼ yard
• for outside border, ½ yard
• for pieced 9-patch blocks and appliqués, assorted scraps
• for star border, ⅓ yard each of 2 contrasting

Notions:
• ¼ yard lightweight fusible webbing
• coordinating thread
• embroidery floss
• fine-tip permanent black pen
• quilting thread

Cutting & Preparation

1. **9-patch Pieced Blocks:** Cut (225) 2½" assorted squares for (25) 9-patch pieced blocks.
2. **Background Blocks:** Cut (24) 6½" light-colored background blocks.
3. **Narrow Border:** Cut (4) 1" x 43" strips.
4. **Checkerboard Border:** Cut (7) 1½" x 21" light-colored strips and (7) 1½" x 21" dark-colored strips.
5. **Pieced Star Border:** Cut (12) 4¼" light-colored squares and (10) 4¼" dark-colored squares.
6. **Outside Border:** Cut (2) 2½" x 43" strips for top and bottom and (4) 2½" x 30" strips for sides.

Appliqués

1. Trace and cut 24 Andy &/or Annie from Appliqué Patterns on page 97 and 12 stars from Garden Patch on page 118, following General Appliqué Instructions on pages 6–7.

Tip: We used a variety of fun fabrics for Andy's features. Use your creativity and enjoy!

2. Using permanent pen, transfer facial features onto Annie and Andy's faces. For noses, fuse a triangle of fabric to face with fusible webbing. To add color, use a cotton swab to apply blush on their cheeks.

3. After facial features have been transferred, center appliqués on background pieces as shown in photo on page 11. Fuse appliqués in place.

4. Machine-appliqué around shapes matching threads to faces.

5. Tear a 1½" x 13" strip of fabric for each Annie's bow. Tie bows and trim ends to desired length. Tack bows in place.

Diagram A

Diagram B

Construction

1. **9-patch Pieced Blocks:** Make (25) 9-patch blocks as shown in Diagram A. With RST, sew 9-patch blocks to appliquéd blocks in 7 rows of 7 blocks, alternating 9-patch blocks and Annie or Andy blocks as shown in Diagram B. With RST, sew rows together, with 9-patch blocks in all 4 corners.

2. **Narrow Border:** With RST, sew 1" x 43" strips to top and bottom of quilt top. Trim excess fabric. With RST, sew 1" x 43" strips to sides of quilt top. Press all seams toward stripping.

3. **Checkerboard Border:** With RST, sew 1½" x 21" strips of fabric together, alternating colors as shown in Diagram C. Cut this into (3) 7" strips. With RST, sew these strips together and cut this piece into (4) 1½" strips as shown in Diagram D.

Diagram C

Diagram D

4. With RST, sew 2 strips together, reversing 1 to make colors opposite as shown in Diagram E. Do this again for 2 checkerboard strips. With RST, sew to top and bottom of quilt top. Press seams toward narrow border.

5. **Pieced Star Border:** Center and fuse a star onto each 4¼" light-colored square. Machine-appliqué around stars. Sew 6 appliquéd star squares to (5) 4¼" dark-colored squares as shown in Diagram B on page 13. Do this again. Sew star borders to top and bottom of quilt top. Trim any excess fabric if necessary. Press seams toward border.

6. **Outside Border:** Sew (2) 2½" x 30" strips together to form a 2½" x 60" strip. Do this again. Sew 2½" x 60" strips to sides of quilt top, trimming off any excess fabric. Press all seams to outside border.

7. **Quilting:** We quilted around the shapes and around the blocks of our quilt, and tied the 9-patch blocks as shown in Diagram F.

8. Finish quilt, following General Finishing Instructions on page 8.

Diagram E

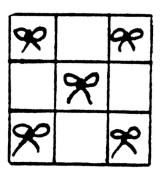

Diagram F

Classic Annie & Andy Pillow

Finished size 18½" x 18½"

Supplies Needed

- 18" pillow form

Batting:

- 23" x 45"

Fabric:

- for appliqué and other parts of pillow, assorted scraps
- for background and backing, ½ yard
- for border, ¼ yard

- for checkerboard, ¼ yard each of light- and dark-colored
- for pillow back, ¾ yard

Notions:

- ¼ yard regular fusible webbing
- embroidery floss (2 complementary colors)
- fine-tip permanent black pen
- quilting thread

Diagram A

Diagram B

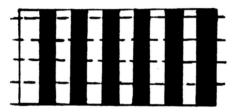

Diagram C

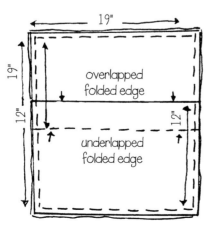

Diagram D

Cutting & Preparation

1. **Pillow Top:** Cut (1) 12½" background square.
2. Cut (4) 5" squares each of fabric and batting.
3. Cut (4) 4" squares of fabric. Center and baste 4" squares onto 5" squares as shown in photo on page 15.
4. **Checkerboard Borders:** Cut (14) 1½" x 7" light-colored strips and (14) 1½" x 7" dark-colored strips.
5. **Stripping:** Cut (2) 1¾" x 19" strips and (2) 1¾" x 16½" strips.
6. **Pillow Back:** Cut (2) 19" x 24" pieces for pillow back.

Appliqués

1. Trace and cut Annie &/or Andy from Appliqué Patterns on pages 97–100, following General Appliqué Instructions on pages 6–7.
2. Using permanent pen, transfer facial features onto Annie and Andy's faces. For noses, fuse triangle of fabric to face with fusible webbing. To add color, use a cotton swab to apply blush on their cheeks.
3. After facial features have been transferred, center appliqués on 5" squares. Fuse appliqués in place as shown in Diagram A or photo on page 15.
4. Pen-stitch around shapes as shown in photo, following General Pen-stitching Instructions on page 9.
5. Tear a 1½" x 13" strip of fabric for Annie's Bow. Tie bow and trim ends to desired length. Tack bow in place.

  16

In Diagram D: 19" (top), 19" (left), 12" (left), 12" (right), overlapped folded edge, underlapped folded edge

Construction

1. Center 5" squares of batting under 5" squares of fabric. Sew 4" squares onto 5" squares of fabric through all 3 layers, using a running stitch, following General Embroidery Instructions on page 7. Pin 5" squares onto pillow top as shown in photo on page 15. Sew around squares, using a running stitch.

2. **Checkerboard Border for Top and Bottom:** With RST, sew (12) 1½" x 7" strips of fabric together, alternating colors as shown in Diagram B on page 16. Cut this into (4) 1½" strips as shown in Diagram C on page 16. With RST, sew 2 strips together, reversing 1 to make colors opposite. Do this again for 2 checkerboard strips. With RST, sew to top and bottom of pillow top. Press seams toward stripping.

3. **Checkerboard Border for Sides:** With RST, sew (16) 1½" x 7" strips of fabric together, alternating colors as shown in Diagram B on page 16. Cut this into (4) 1½" strips as shown in Diagram C on page 16. With RST, sew 2 strips together, reversing 1 to make colors opposite. Do this again for 2 checkerboard strips. With RST, sew to sides of pillow top. Press seams toward stripping.

4. **Outside Stripping:** With RST, sew 1¾" x 16½" strips to top and bottom of pillow top. Press seams toward stripping. Sew 1¾" x 19" strips to sides of pillow top. Trim any excess fabric. Press seams toward stripping.

5. **Batting:** Cut a square of backing and a square of batting the same size as pillow top. Layer batting between wrong side of pillow top and backing. Baste through all layers. Quilt around shapes and checkerboard border.

6. **Pillow Back:** Fold 19" x 24" pieces in half, forming (2) 12" x 19" pieces. Press to set crease. Overlap folded edges so that pillow back is same size as pillow front. Pin and baste all raw edges together as shown in Diagram D on page 16. With RST, pin and sew pillow front to pillow back. Clip corners and turn right side out.

7. Insert pillow form.

Annie & Andy Wall Pictures

Finished size 11½" x 18½"

Supplies Needed

Batting:
- 18" x 45"

Fabric:
- for background and backing,
  ½ yard light-colored
- for patched border and appliqués,
  assorted scraps
- for stripping, ¼ yard

Notions:
- ¼ yard regular fusible webbing
- embroidery floss (optional)
- fine-tip permanent black pen

Cutting & Preparation

1. **Background:** Cut (1) 8" x 15" background piece for each wall picture.
2. **Narrow Border:** Cut (2) 1" x 8" strips and (2) 1" x 16" strips for each wall picture.
3. **Pieced Border:** Cut (8) 2⅝" squares for top and bottom of each picture. With RST, sew (4) 2⅝" squares to form a 2⅝" x 9" strip. Do this again for another 4-square strip. Cut (20) 2½" squares for sides of each picture. With RST, sew (10) 2½" squares to form a 2½" x 20½" strip. Do this again for another 10-square strip.

Construction

1. **Narrow Border:** With RST, sew 1" x 8" strips to top and bottom of background as shown in Diagram A. With RST, sew 1" x 16" strips to sides of background. Press all seams toward stripping.

2. **Pieced Border:** With RST, sew 4-section strips to top and bottom of picture. Trim off any excess length from ends. With RST, sew 10-square strips to sides (don't worry about matching squares at the corners). Trim off any excess length. Press seams toward pieced border.

Appliqués

1. Trace and cut Annie and Andy from Appliqué Patterns on pages 98–99 as you desire, following General Appliqué Instructions on pages 6–7.

2. Using permanent pen, transfer facial features onto Annie and Andy's faces. For noses, fuse a triangle of fabric to face with fusible webbing. To add color, use a cotton swab to apply blush on their cheeks.

3. After facial features have been transferred, center appliqués onto background piece as shown in photo on page 18. Fuse appliqués in place.

4. Pen-stitch around shapes as shown in photo on page 18, following General Pen-stitching Instructions on page 9.

5. Tear a 1½" x 13" strip of fabric for Annie's bow. Tie bow and trim ends to desired length. Tack bow in place.

Running Stitch

Diagram A

Quilting Instructions

1. Cut a piece of batting and a piece of backing slightly larger than wall picture. Place batting between wrong side of picture and backing. Pin securely in place.

2. Using 3 strands of embroidery floss, sew ¼" inside stripping with a running stitch as shown in Diagram A, following General Embroidery Instructions on page 7.

3. Quilt around outside edges of appliqué, narrow border, and pieced border.

Finishing

Note: Your picture is ready to frame. Our frame is 14" x 21" with an 11" x 18" opening. If you are not planning to frame your wall picture, then bind, following General Finishing Instructions on page 8.

1. Trim the edges of your picture to fit your size of frame.

2. Sew outside raw edges of picture together with a zigzag stitch before framing.

Garden Wall Quilt

Finished size 21½" x 24"

Cutting & Preparation

1. **Garden Blocks:** Cut a block to dimensions for each Garden shape used from Appliqué Patterns on pages 100–106 plus ¼" on all sides for background blocks as shown in photo on page 20.
2. **1st Border:** Cut (2) 1" x 17¾" strips for top and bottom and (2) 1" x 19½" strips for sides.
3. **Outside Border:** Cut (2) 2¼" x 20½" strips for top and bottom and (2) 2¼" x 21" strips for sides.

Appliqués

1. Trace and cut Garden shapes from Appliqué Patterns on page 100–106 as shown in photo on page 20.
2. Fuse appliqués onto centers of appropriate background blocks with fusible webbing.
3. Using black permanent pen, pen-stitch around shapes, following General Pen-stitching Instructions on page 9.
4. Add details to appliqués. To add color, use a cotton swab to apply blush to girl's cheeks and red permanent pen to her lips.

Supplies Needed

Batting:
• 24" x 45"

Fabric:
• for backgrounds and appliqués, assorted scraps
• for backing, ¾ yard
• for binding, ¼ yard
• for outside border, ⅓ yard
• for stripping, ⅛ yard

Notions:
• 1 yard regular fusible webbing
• fine-tip permanent black pen
• fine-tip permanent red pen
• quilting thread

Diagram A

Construction

1. With RST, sew all background blocks together as shown in Diagram A.
2. **1st Border:** With RST, sew 1" x 17¾" strips to top and bottom of quilt top and 1" x 19½" strips to sides of quilt top.
3. **Outside Border:** With RST, sew 2¼" x 20½" strips to top and bottom of quilt top and 2¼" x 21" strips to sides of quilt top.
4. Finish quilt, following General Finishing Instructions on page 8.

Bloomin' Bunnies Gift Bags

Finished size 8" x 6¼"

Supplies Needed

Batting:

• 9" x 45"

Fabric:

• for appliqués and handle, assorted scraps

• for bag and lining, ⅝ yard

Notions:

• ¼ yard regular fusible webbing

• (4) ⅝" buttons

• embroidery floss

• fine-tip permanent black pen

• for handles, (20") 18-gauge wire

Cutting & Preparation

1. Cut (2) 8½" x 13½" pieces for bag and bag lining, (1) 5¼" x 7½" piece for background rectangle, (1) 5¼" x 7½" piece of batting, and (1) 4¼" x 6½" piece for inner rectangle.

2. **Handles:** Tear (2) ¾" x 11½" strips. With WST, fold each in half lengthwise and sew down length approximately ⅛" from raw edges, forming casing on one side as shown in Diagram A.

3. With WST, fold bag in half widthwise to form a front and back. Press to form crease. Do this again for bag lining.

Diagram A

4. Layer and pin batting, background rectangle, and inner rectangle on bag front ¾" from upper edge. Sew ¼" from edges of background rectangle and inner rectangle through all layers with a running stitch as shown in Diagram B, following General Embroidery Instructions on page 7.

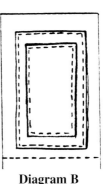

Diagram B

Appliqués

1. Trace and cut Garden shapes from Appliqué Patterns on pages 106–107 as you desire, following General Appliqué Instructions on pages 6–7.
2. Fuse shapes and/or letters onto center of background rectangle with fusible webbing as shown in photo on page 22.
3. For watermelon bag, cut (7) 1" squares each of black and white for checkerboard border.
4. For watermelon bag, alternate black and white 1" squares and fuse onto lower section of inner square as shown in photo on page 22, before fusing watermelon onto inner rectangle.
5. Using permanent pen, pen-stitch around shapes, following General Pen-stitching Instructions on page 9.

Construction

1. With RST, sew side seams of bag. Sew side seams of lining, leaving a 2" opening in one side of lining for turning as shown in Diagram C.
2. With RST, sew bag to lining at upper edge.
3. Turn bag right side out through side opening in lining. Hand-stitch opening shut.
4. **Handles:** Cut (2) 9" lengths of wire. Insert wires through handle casings. Fold under ends of casing ½" on both ends to cover. Sew ends of handle to front and back of bag as shown in Diagram D.
5. Sew buttons to top of bag to cover wire ends.

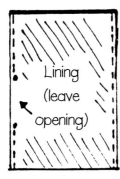

Diagram C

23

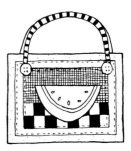

Diagram D

Bloomin' Bunnies Wall Quilt

Finished size 26½" x 36½"

Cutting & Preparation

1. **Bunny Blocks:** Cut (6) 6½" x 8¾" light-colored background blocks.

2. **Flower and Vegetable Blocks:** Cut (6) 3" x 6½" background blocks.

3. **Stripping:** Cut (15) 1½" x 6½" strips for top and bottom of blocks.

4. **Stripping:** Cut (4) 1½" x 3" strips, (4) 1½" x 4" strips, and (8) 1½" x 10¾" strips for sides of flower and vegetable blocks.

5. **Background:** Cut (1) 4" x 19½" rectangle and (1) 6" x 22½" rectangle for word backgrounds.

6. **Outside Border:** Cut (2) 2½" x 26½" strips for top and bottom of quilt top and (2) 2½" x 33" strips for sides of quilt top.

Appliqués

1. Trace and cut Bunny and Garden shapes and words from Appliqué Patterns on pages 106–111 following General Appliqué Instructions on pages 6–7.

2. Fuse bunnies onto 6½" x 8¾" blocks, flowers and vegetables onto 3" x 6½" blocks, and words onto 4" x 19½" background with fusible webbing as shown in photo on page 24.

3. Using black permanent pen, pen-stitch around shapes as desired, following General Pen-stitching Instructions on page 9.

Hoe, Hoe, Hoe,
to the garden we go.
Hop, Hop, Hop,
it's our favorite stop!
Spring has sprung and here is
the project to get you going!
You're sure to dig this delight-
ful quilt.

Supplies Needed

Batting:
- 36" x 45"

Fabric:
- for appliqués and stripping, assorted scraps (if purchasing, buy quarter yards)
- for wording background, ¼ yard each of 2 contrasting
- for backing, 1 yard
- for binding, ⅓ yard
- for outside border, ½ yard

Notions:
- 2 yards regular fusible webbing
- embroidery floss
- fine-tip permanent black pen

Construction

1. With RST, sew (1) 1½" x 6½" strip to top and bottom of each bunny block as shown in Diagram A. Press seams toward stripping.

2. With RST, sew (4) 1½" x 10¾" strips to 3 bunny blocks for a row of bunnies. Do this again for 2 rows of bunnies. Press seams toward stripping.

3. With RST, sew (4) 1½" x 3" strips to sides of (3) 3" x 6½" flower and vegetable blocks for 3" x 18½" strip. Press seams toward stripping.

4. With RST, sew 1½" x 6½" strips to bottom of remaining flower and vegetable blocks. Press seams toward stripping.

5. With RST, sew (4) 1½" x 4" strips to sides of flower and vegetable blocks for 4" x 18½" strip. Press seams toward stripping.

6. With RST, sew 3" x 18½" strip to bottom of 1 row of bunnies and 4" x 18½" strip to bottom of remaining row of bunnies as shown in Diagram B. Press seams toward stripping.

7. With RST, sew bunnies with stripping together with 4" x 18½" stripping on bottom.

8. With RST, sew 6" x 22½" word background to bottom 4" x 18½" strip.

9. Center and sew 4" x 19½" word background to top of 6" x 22½" word background with a running stitch and embroidery floss, following General Embroidery Instructions on page 7.

10. With RST, sew 2½" x 26½" border to top and bottom of quilt top and 2½" x 33" outside border to sides of quilt top. Press seams toward border.

11. Finish quilt, following General Finishing Instructions on page 8.

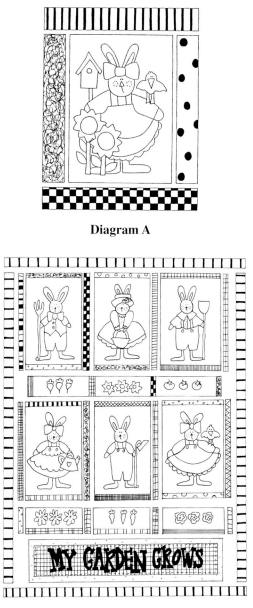

Diagram A

Diagram B

Bloomin' Bunnies Wall Pictures

Finished size 6" x 8½"

Cutting & Preparation

1. **Background:** Cut (1) 6½" x 8¾" light-colored background piece for each wall picture.
2. **Border:** Cut (2) 1½" x 6½" strips and (2) 1½" x 8¾" strips for each wall picture.

Supplies Needed

Batting:
• 9" x 45"

Fabric:
• for appliqués and stripping, assorted scraps
• for background, ¼ yard light-colored

Notions:
• ¼ yard regular fusible webbing
• fine-tip permanent black pen

Appliqués

1. Trace and cut Bunny and Garden shapes from Appliqué Patterns on pages 107–111 as you desire, following General Appliqué Instructions on pages 6–7.
2. Using permanent pen, transfer faces onto appliqués.
3. Center and fuse appliqués onto background fabrics as shown in photo on page 27.
4. Pen-stitch around shapes, following General Pen-stitching Instructions on page 9.

Diagram A

Construction

1. **Border:** With RST, sew 1½" x 6½" strips to sides of background piece as shown in Diagram A.
2. With RST, sew 1½" x 8¾" strips to top and bottom of background piece. Press seams toward stripping.

Quilting Instructions

1. Cut a piece of batting and a piece of backing slightly larger than wall picture. Place batting between wrong side of picture and backing. Pin securely in place.
2. Quilt around outside edges of appliqué and stripping.

Finishing

Note: Your picture is ready to frame. Our frame is 10½" x 12½" with an 8" x 10" opening. If you are not planning to frame your wall picture, then bind, following General Finishing Instructions on page 8.

1. Trim the edges of your picture to fit your size of frame.
2. Sew outside raw edges of picture together with a zigzag stitch before framing.

29

Barnyard Wall Quilt

Finished size 31" x 31"

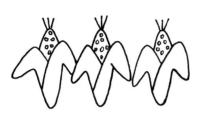

Fresh from the farm comes our friendly cow, pig, sheep, and barn wall quilt. These fashionable fellows are fun to sew and are sure to please the kids you know.

Supplies Needed

Batting:
• 35" x 45"

Fabric:
• for 1st border and stripping, ¼ yard
• for 2nd border, ¼ yard
• for 3rd border, ⅓ yard brown and ¼ yard green
• for 4th border, ½ yard
• for animal and barn blocks, assorted fabrics
• for backing, 1 yard
• for binding, ⅓ yard

Notions:
• ½ yard lightweight fusible webbing

Cutting & Preparation

1. Cut 1 each of Templates 1–4 on pages 34–36 for each animal as you desire, adding ¼" all around and following instructions on templates.

2. Cut 5 of Template 5 on page 35 for each animal. With RST, fold along dashed lines and press to form crease. Fold in half lengthwise again and press. Sew along folded edges.

3. Trim ⅛" off length of 1 strip for each animal and tie knot in one end, forming a tail. Tie knot in one end of each remaining strip, forming legs.

4. Pin legs' inside seam allowance to right side of grass (Template 2), matching each leg to dot on template. If making girl cow, trace and cut Udder from Barnyard Appliqué Patterns on page 112. Center and fuse onto grass with fusible webbing as shown on Template 2. Baste legs in place.

Note: Girl cow leg placement differs from boy cow, sheep, and pig to allow for udder.

5. Pin tail's inside seam allowance to right side of body (Template 1), matching tail to dot on template. Baste tail in place.

6. With RST, sew each animal block as shown in Diagram A on page 31.

7. Cut 1 of Templates 2 and 6–11 on pages 34–37 for barn, following instructions on templates.

8. With RST, sew barn pieces 6–11 together as shown in Diagram B. Clip piece 7 to dot.

9. **Stripping:** Cut (4) 2½" x 8½" strips and (1) 2½" square.

10. **1st Border:** Cut (2) 2" x 16¾" strips for top and bottom and (2) 2" x 19¾" strips for sides.

11. **2nd Border:** Cut (2) 1¼" x 19¾" strips for top and bottom of quilt top and (2) 1¼" x 21¼" strips for sides of quilt top.

12. **3rd Border:** Cut (6) 1¼" x 44" brown strips for fence and fence post and (4) 1¾" x 44" green strips for background behind fence.

13. **4th Border:** Cut (2) 2" x 27½" strips for top and bottom and (2) 2" x 32½" strips for sides.

14. **Binding:** Cut (4) 2½" x 44" strips.

15. **Fence Corners**: Cut (4) 1¾" green background squares, (4) 1¾" x 2½" green background rectangles, (4) 1¾" x 3¾" green background rectangles, (4) 1¼" x 1¾" brown fence pieces, and (4) 1¼" x 2" brown fence pieces.

Appliqués

1. Trace and cut Barnyard shapes from Appliqué Patterns on page 112 as you desire, following General Appliqué Instructions on pages 6–7.

2. Center and fuse animal faces onto appropriate body.

3. Fuse door, roof, window, and hay onto barn as shown in Diagram C.

4. Machine-appliqué around all pieces.

5. Using black permanent pen, apply dots for eyes on animals.

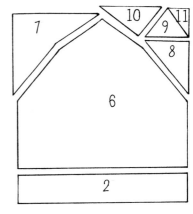

Diagram B

Diagram A

Diagram C

Diagram D

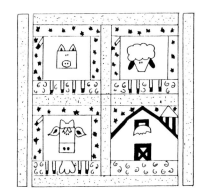

Diagram E

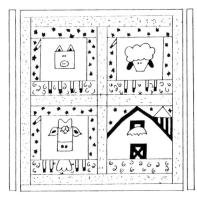

Diagram F

Construction

1. With RST, sew grass (Template 2) to bottom of barn block.
2. Arrange Barnyard blocks in rows of 2 as you desire.
3. Working with the top row of 2 blocks and with RST, sew (1) 2½" x 8½" strip between 2 blocks to form a row. Do this again with bottom row of blocks as shown in Diagram D.
4. With RST, sew 2½" square between (2) 2½" x 8½" strips for horizontal stripping.
5. With RST, sew horizontal stripping between top and bottom rows of blocks.
6. **1st Border:** With RST, sew 2" x 16¾" strips to top and bottom of quilt top and 2" x 19¾" strips to sides of quilt top as shown in Diagram E. Press all seams away from quilt center.
7. **2nd Border:** With RST, sew 1¼" x 19¾" strips to top and bottom of quilt top and 1¼" x 21¼" strips to sides of quilt top as shown in Diagram F. Press all seams away from quilt center.
8. **3rd Border (Fence):** Cut (4) 1¼" x 44" strips into (10) 1¼" x 4" strips for 40 fence posts as shown in Diagram G on page 33. You will have extra from each strip.
9. With RST, sew (1) 1¼" x 44" brown strip between (2) 1¾" x 44" green strips. Cut this into (18) 2" x 4" sections as shown in Diagram H on page 33. Do this again for 36 fence and grass sections.
10. With RST, sew 10 fence posts to 9 fence and grass sections, beginning and ending

with a fence post as shown in Diagram I. Do this again for 4 fence strips.

11. With RST, sew fence strips to top and bottom of quilt top as shown in Diagram J.

12. **Fence Corners:** With RST, sew fence corners together as shown in Diagram K.

13. With RST, sew fence corner to each side of remaining fence strips as shown in Diagram J, matching corner cross bars for continuous fence rail.

14. With RST, sew remaining fence strips to sides of quilt top. Press all seams on fence border toward fence so it will stand out.

15. **4th Border:** With RST, sew 2" x 27½" strips to top and bottom of quilt top and 2" x 32½" strips to sides of quilt top as shown in Diagram L. Press seams away from quilt center.

16. Finish quilt, following General Finishing Instructions on page 8.

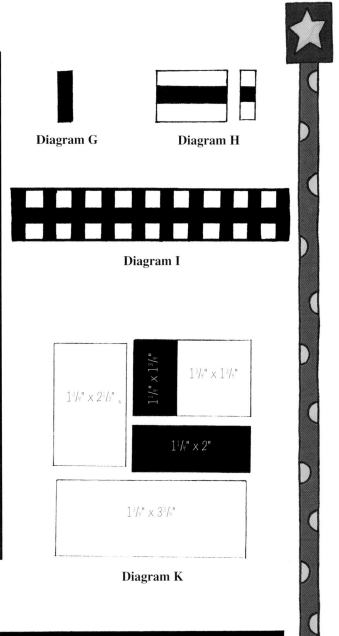

Diagram G   **Diagram H**

Diagram I

1³/₄" x 2½"   1¼" x 1³/₄"   1³/₄" x 1³/₄"

1¼" x 2"

1³/₄" x 3³/₄"

Diagram K

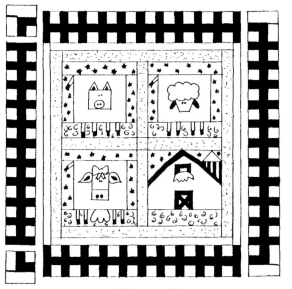

Diagram J

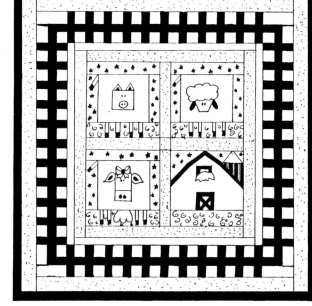

Diagram L

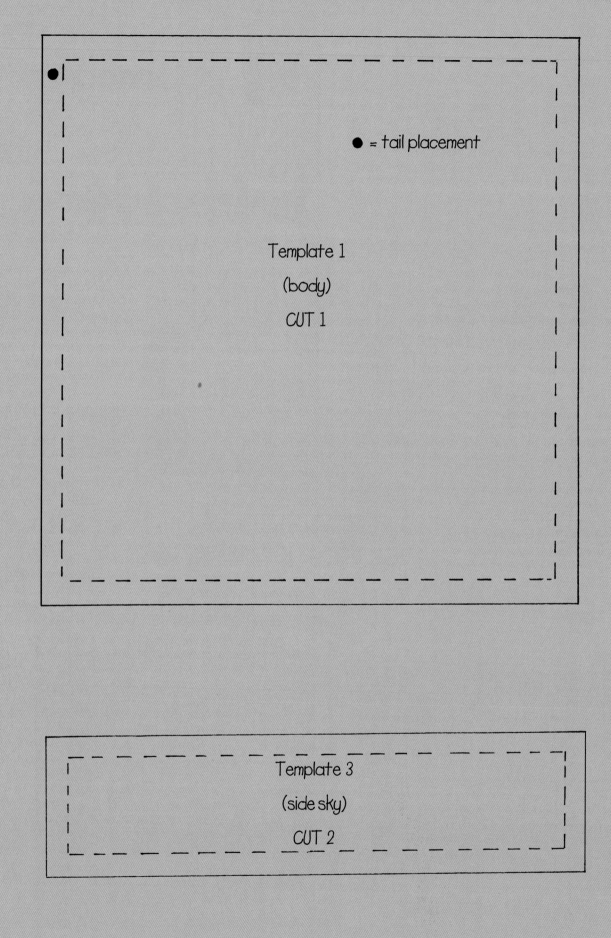

● = tail placement

Template 1

(body)

CUT 1

Template 3

(side sky)

CUT 2

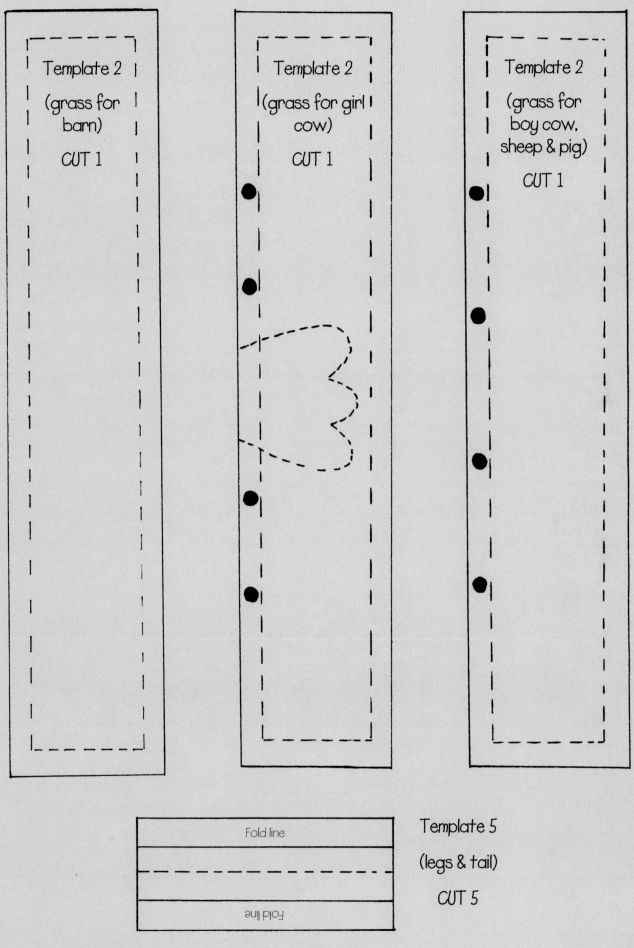

Template 2

(grass for barn)

CUT 1

Template 2

(grass for girl cow)

CUT 1

Fold line

Template 2

(grass for boy cow, sheep & pig)

CUT 1

Fold line

Fold line

Template 5

(legs & tail)

CUT 5

35

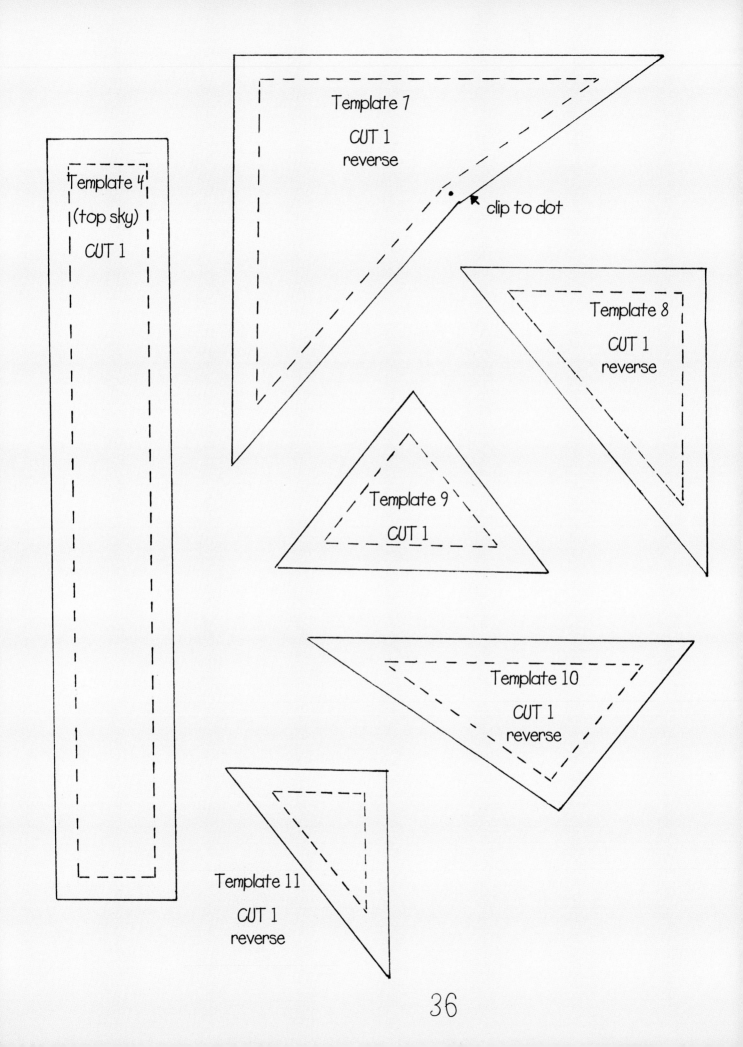

Template 7

CUT 1
reverse

clip to dot

Template 4
(top sky)
CUT 1

Template 8

CUT 1
reverse

Template 9

CUT 1

Template 10

CUT 1
reverse

Template 11

CUT 1
reverse

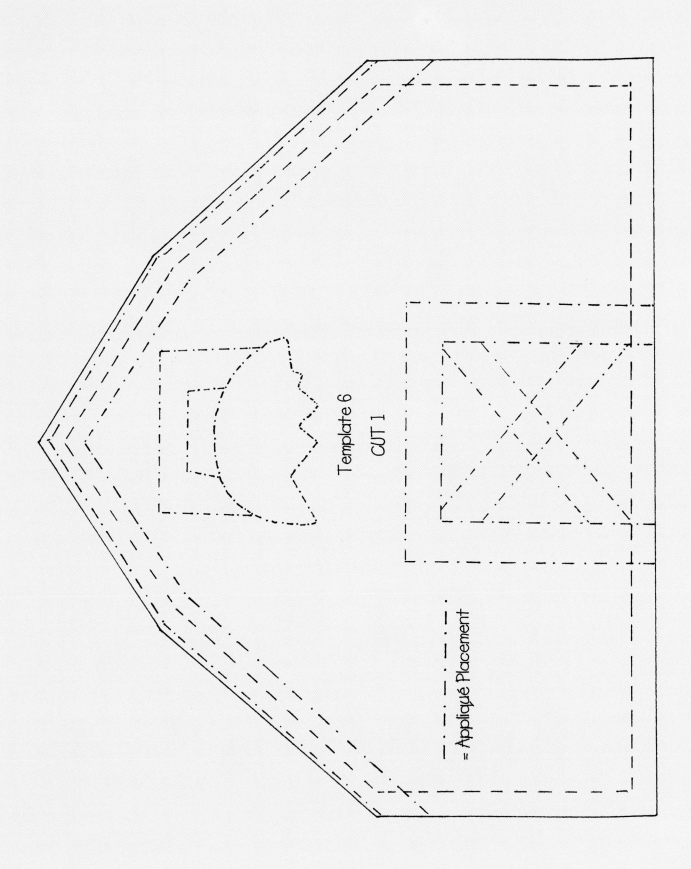

Template 6

CUT 1

-·-· = Appliqué Placement

38

Baby Bear Quilt

Finished size 40" x 50"

Cutting & Preparation

1. **Bear Blocks:** Cut (12) 7½" background blocks.
2. **Stripping Between Blocks:** Cut (17) 1½" x 7½" strips to go between blocks.
3. Corner Posts: Cut (6) 1½" squares for corner posts between stripping.
4. **1st Border:** Cut (2) 1½" x 25½" strips for top and bottom and (2) 1½" x 31½" strips for sides.
5. **2nd & 3rd Borders:** Cut (174) 3" light- and dark-colored squares.
6. **Binding:** Cut (5) 2½" x 44" strips.

Appliqués

1. Trace and cut 12 Bear shapes from Appliqué Patterns on page 112 as you desire, following General Appliqué Instructions on pages 6–7.
2. Fuse appliqués to center of 7½" squares with fusible webbing as shown in photo on page 38.
3. Machine-appliqué or blanket stitch around shapes.

Construction

1. Arrange 7½" blocks as you desire as shown in Diagram A.
2. Working with the top row and with RST, sew (2) 1½" x 7½" strips between 3 blocks

This is a fun way to show your creativity by using lots of different fabrics.

Supplies Needed

Batting:
• 45" x 50"

Fabric:
• for 1st border, ¼ yard
• for backing, 1½ yards
• for background squares, ¾ yard
• for binding, ½ yard
• for patchwork border and appliqués, assorted scraps
• for stripping, ¼ yard

Notions:
• 1¼ yards lightweight fusible webbing
• for appliqués, coordinating thread

Diagram A

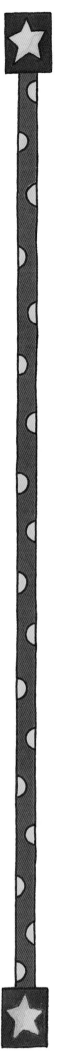

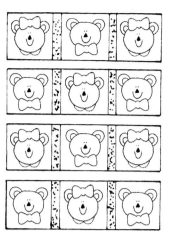

Diagram B

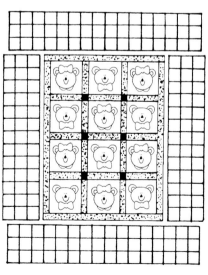

Diagram C

to form a row as shown in Diagram B. Do this again for remaining rows.

3. **Horizontal Stripping:** With RST, sew (2) 1½" squares and (3) 1½" x 7½" strips together as shown in Diagram C. Do this again for 3 strips. Sew strips horizontally between each row of blocks.

4. **1st Border:** With RST, sew 1½" x 31½" strips to sides of quilt top. With RST, sew 1½" x 25½" strips to top and bottom of quilt top. Press seams toward border.

5. **2nd Border:** With RST, sew (13) 3" squares together forming a long strip. Do this again for (6) 13-square strips. With RST, sew (3) 13-square strips together lengthwise for 2 side borders as shown in Diagram D. With RST, sew borders to sides of quilt top.

6. **3rd Border:** With RST, sew (16) 3" squares together, forming a long strip. Do this again for (6) 16-square strips. With RST, sew (3) 16-square strips together lengthwise for top and bottom borders. With RST, sew top and bottom borders to quilt top.

7. Finish quilt, following General Finishing Instructions on page 8.

Diagram D

Fun & Friendly Bug Quilt

Vivid colors and happy shapes make this a positively perfect project for all your "bug-loving" friends!

Supplies Needed

Batting:

• 72" x 90"

Fabric:

• for 1st border, 1¼ yards for 2nd border, 1¼ yards (This allows for cutting 8 strips and sewing together to make 4 border strips. If you want to piece your border strips more, you can buy less yardage.)

• for background blocks, 2½ yards light-colored

• for backing, 5⅓ yards

• for binding, ¾ yard

• for bug appliqués, pieced 3rd border, and stripping around each 10½" block, assorted scraps (if purchasing, buy quarter yards)

• for contrasting posts between stripping, ⅓ yard

• for stripping, 1¼ yards

Notions:

• 6 yards lightweight fusible webbing

• dark brown embroidery floss

• for appliqués, coordinating thread

Finished size 72" x 86"

Cutting & Preparation

1. **Bug Blocks:** Cut (20) 10½" background blocks.

2. **Stripping Around Blocks:** Cut (2) 1½" x 10½" strips and (2) 1½" x 12½" strips to go around each 10½" block. We used a different color for each block.

3. **Stripping Between Blocks:** Cut (34) 2½" x 12½" strips to go between blocks.

4. **Corner Posts:** Cut (30) 2½" squares for corner posts between stripping.

5. **1st Border:** Cut (8) 2" x 45" strips. With RST, sew to form (4) 2" x 90" strips. From these 4 strips, cut (2) 2" x 72½" strips and (2) 2" x 61½" strips.

6. **2nd Border:** Cut (8) 1" x 45" strips. With RST, sew to form (4) 1" x 90" strips. From these 4 strips, cut (2) 1" x 75½" strips and (2) 1" x 62½" strips.

7. **Pieced 3rd Border:** Cut (40) 5¼" x 7½" colorful rectangles. With RST, sew 9 rectangles into a strip along 5¼" sides. Do this again for another 9-rectangle strip. Each 9-section strip should measure 5½" x 62" finished. Trim or seam out excess length to this measurement. With RST, sew 11 rectangles into a strip along 5¼" sides. Do this again for another 11-rectangle strip. Each 11-rectangle strip should measure 5¼" x 76½" finished. Trim or seam out excess length to this measurement. Cut (4) 5¼" squares for corners of border.

8. **Binding:** Cut (8) 2½" x 45" strips.

Appliqués

1. Trace and cut 20 Bug shapes from Appliqué Patterns on pages 114–118 for blocks as you desire, following General Appliqué Instructions on page 6.

2. Fuse appliqués to center of background blocks with fusible webbing as shown in photo on page 41.

3. Machine-appliqué or blanket stitch around shapes.

4. Transfer and embroider antennas, eyes, and legs on bugs, following General Embroidery Instructions on page 7.

Construction

1. With RST, sew (2) 1½" x 10½" strips to sides of each block as shown in Diagram A. With RST, sew (2) 1½" x 13" strips to top and bottom of each block. Press seams toward stripping.

2. Lay out blocks in rows of 4 as you desire. With RST, sew 2½" x 12½" strips between 4 blocks as shown in Diagram B. Do this again for 5 rows. Press seams toward stripping.

3. With RST, sew (4) 2½" x 12½" strips and 5 corner posts together, forming 1 long strip as shown in Diagram C. Do this again for 6 strips. Press seams toward stripping.

4. With RST, sew strips between assembled quilt sections as shown in Diagram D. Press seams toward stripping.

Diagram A

Diagram B

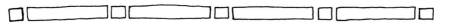

Diagram C

Diagram D

5. **1st Border:** With RST, sew 2" x 61½" strips to top and bottom of quilt top. With RST, sew 2" x 72½" strips to sides of quilt top as shown in Diagram E. Press seams toward quilt center.

6. **2nd Border:** With RST, sew 1" x 61½" strips to top and bottom of quilt top. With RST, sew 1" x 75½" strips to sides of quilt top. Press seams toward quilt center.

7. **Pieced 3rd Border:** With RST, sew 11-rectangle strips to sides of quilt top. With RST, sew (1) 5¼" square to each end of 9-rectangle strips. With RST, sew 9-rectangle strips to top and bottom of quilt top. Press seams toward quilt center.

8. Finish quilt, following General Finishing Instructions on page 8.

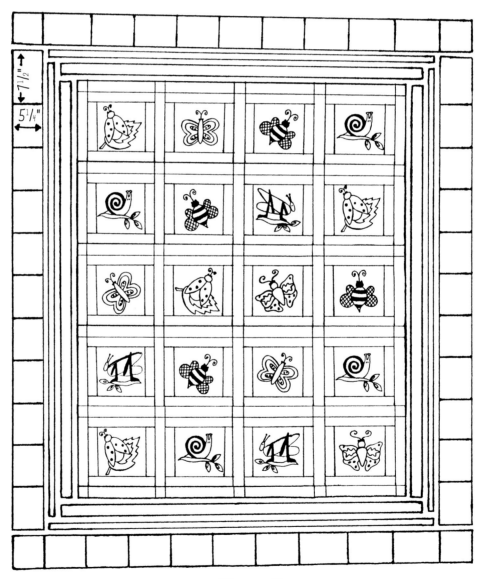

Diagram E

Fun & Friendly Bug Pillow

Finished size 16" x 16"

To add color and cheer to any room, sew up piles of these playful pillows. They make great gifts, too!

Supplies Needed

- 16" pillow form

Batting:

- 21" x 45"

Fabric:

- for appliqués, assorted scraps
- for background and backing, ½ yard light-colored
- for borders and stripping around pillow, assorted scraps (if purchasing, buy ¼ yard)
- for pillow back, ⅔ yard

Notions:

- ¼ yard regular fusible interfacing
- ¼ yard lightweight fusible webbing
- 2¼ yards piping
- (3) ⅜" buttons
- for appliqués, coordinating thread
- dark brown embroidery floss

Cutting & Preparation

1. **Pillow Top:** Cut (1) 10½" light-colored background square.
2. **1st Border:** Cut (2) 1½" x 10½" strips for sides and (2) 1½" x 12½" strips for top and bottom.
3. **2nd Border:** Cut (2) 2½" x 12½" strips for sides and (2) 2½" x 16½" strips for top and bottom.
4. **Pillow Back:** Cut (2) 16½" x 19½" pieces for pillow back and (2) 2½" x 9" strips of interfacing for pillow back.

Appliqués

1. Trace and cut Bug shape from Appliqué Patterns on pages 114–118 as you desire, following General Appliqué Instructions on pages 6–7.
2. Fuse appliqué to center of pillow top as shown in Diagram A and photo on page 45.
3. Machine-appliqué or blanket stitch around shape.
4. Transfer and embroider antennas, eyes, and legs onto bug, following General Embroidery Instructions on page 7.

Diagram A

Construction

1. **Pillow Top:** With RST, sew 1½" x 10½" strips to sides of pillow top as shown in Diagram B on page 47. With RST, sew

46

1½" x 12½" strips to top and bottom of pillow top. With RST, sew 2½" x 12½" strips to sides of pillow top. With RST, sew 2½" x 16½" strips to top and bottom of pillow top. Press all seams toward stripping.

2. **Batting:** Cut a square of backing and a square of batting the same size as pillow top. Layer batting between wrong side of pillow top and backing. Baste through all layers. Quilt around shapes and borders.

3. **Piping:** Pin piping to right side of pillow top with raw edges together. Slightly round corners of pillow top. Clip piping at corners for ease in sewing as shown in Diagram C. Sew as close as possible to cording so existing stitching line does not show on pillow front.

Note: To hand-make piping, see General Sewing Instructions on pages 8–9.

4. **Pillow Back:** Fold (2) 16½" x 19½" pieces of fabric in half, forming (2) 9¾" x 16½" pieces. Press to set crease. Fuse interfacing to wrong side of pillow backs along folded edge.

5. **Buttonholes and Buttons:** Mark ⅝" buttonholes on one of the backs, starting 3" from each side and center 3 buttonholes as shown in Diagram D. Overlap folded edges so pillow back is same size as pillow front. Mark where buttons go, and sew buttonholes. Sew buttons onto other pillow back, matching to buttonholes.

6. Pin and baste all raw edges together. With RST, pin pillow front to pillow back. Sew in place from pillow back side, following piping stitching line. Clip corners and turn right side out.

7. Insert pillow form.

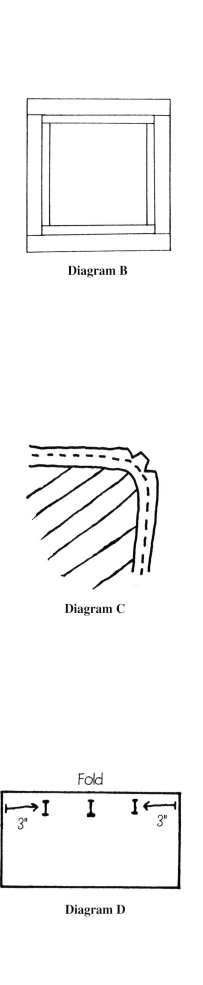

Diagram B

Diagram C

Fold

3"   3"

Diagram D

47

49

Little Sprouts Baby Vest

Sizes: 6M–4T

Make a dapper and fashionable vest for the "Little Sprout" that you love best. This pattern is terrifically fun to sew and offers many opportunities to be creative. You can make a different vest for every season.

Supplies Needed

Fabric:
- for back, ⅜ yard (6M–3T),
    ½ yard (4T)
- for front, ½ yard flannel (for all sizes)
- for lining, ½ yard (for all sizes)
- for piecing vest fronts and appliqués, assorted scraps (for all sizes)

Notions:
- ¼ yard lightweight fusible webbing
- (2) ¾" buttons
- for all fabrics, neutral-colored thread
- for appliqués, coordinating thread

Cutting & Preparation

1. **Vest Fronts:** Cut 2 Vest Fronts on page 52 from unwashed flannel, following Enlarging Patterns from a Grid on page 6. Do this again for lining. Cut assorted sizes of squares and rectangles (1½"–3½") from scraps.

2. Lay the assorted rectangles on the vest fronts, overlapping slightly to cover flannel completely. Starting in the center of the vest, pin each rectangle securely to flannel until flannel is completely covered. Trim off any excess fabric around outside edges of vest fronts. Beginning in the center of vest, sew closely around edges of each rectangle.

3. **Vest Back:** Cut 1 Vest Back on page 52. Do this again for lining.

Construction

1. With RST, pin vest front to vest back at shoulder seams and sew as shown in Diagram A. Press seam open. Do this again for lining.

2. Press under seam allowance on side seams on front and back lining. With RST, pin vest to vest lining and sew, leaving side seams open as shown in Diagram A. Trim seams. Clip curves and trim corners. Turn right side out through one side opening and press.

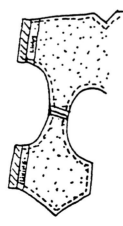

Diagram A

3. With RST, pin side seams together and sew as shown in Diagram B. Be careful not to catch lining. Trim and press seam open. Sew lining closed over seam with a whipstitch.

4. Crazy-stitch over vest fronts, following General Sewing Instructions on pages 8–9. Cover all areas so that lining and flannel are securely attached to vest front. Wash and dry vest (in dryer). This will slightly shrink and "age" the vest.

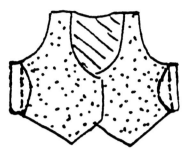

Diagram B

Appliqués

1. Trace and cut Garden Patch shapes from Appliqué Patterns on pages 118–123 for vest as you desire, following General Appliqué Instructions on pages 6–7.

2. Fuse appliqués onto vest with fusible webbing.

3. Machine-appliqué around shapes.

We appliquéd a carrot, tomato, and radish. Feel free to use any appliqués as you desire. It is also fun to put appliqués on the back of vest.

Finishing

1. Topstitch ¼" from edge all around vest and armholes.

2. Make (2) ¾" buttonholes on right vest front for girls or left vest front for boys. Sew on buttons.

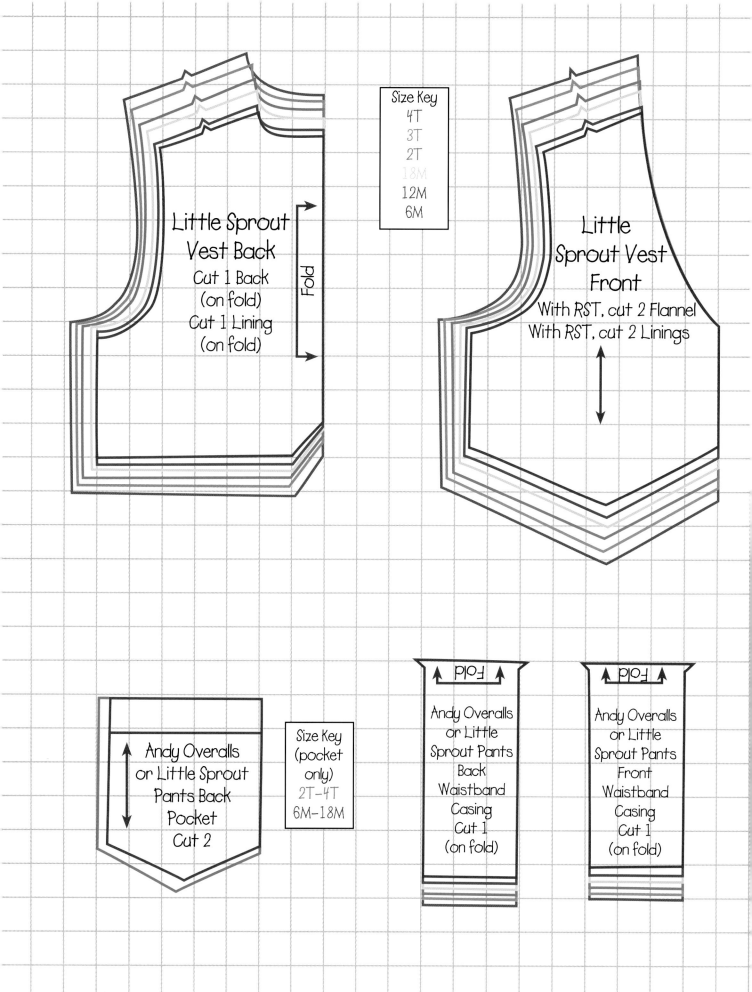

Little Sprout
Vest Back

Cut 1 Back
(on fold)
Cut 1 Lining
(on fold)

Fold

Size Key
4T
3T
2T
18M
12M
6M

Little
Sprout Vest
Front

With RST, cut 2 Flannel
With RST, cut 2 Linings

Andy Overalls
or Little Sprout
Pants Back
Pocket
Cut 2

Size Key
(pocket
only)
2T-4T
6M-18M

Fold

Andy Overalls
or Little
Sprout Pants
Back
Waistband
Casing
Cut 1
(on fold)

Fold

Andy Overalls
or Little
Sprout Pants
Front
Waistband
Casing
Cut 1
(on fold)

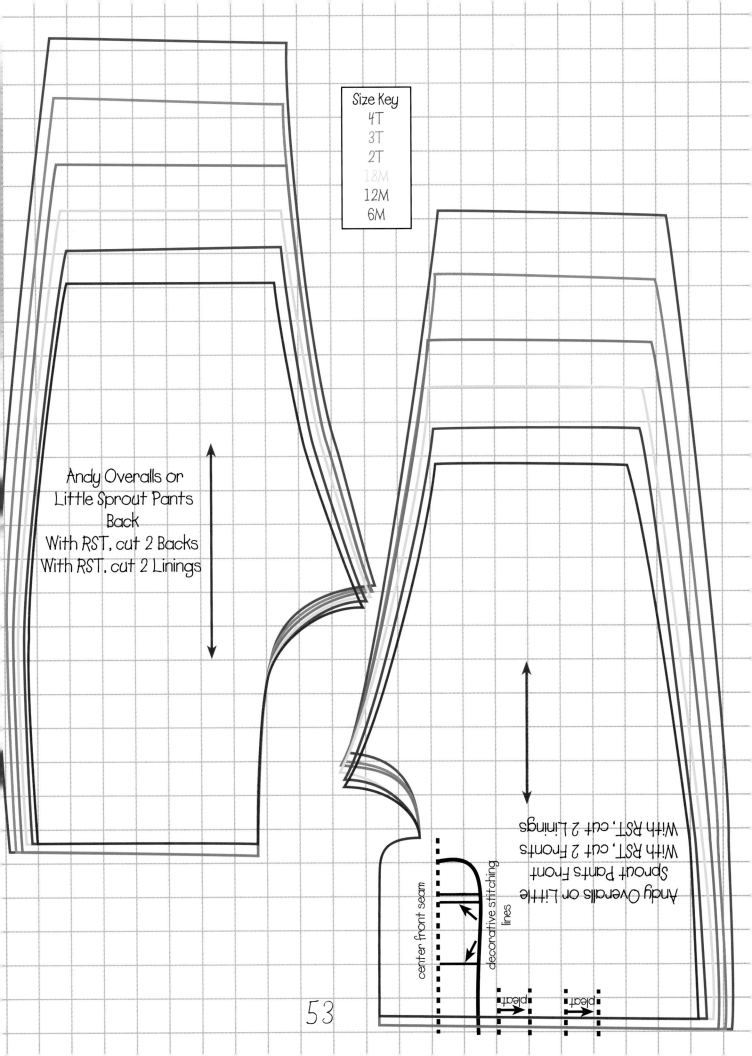

Size Key
4T
3T
2T
18M
12M
6M

Andy Overalls or
Little Sprout Pants
Back
With RST, cut 2 Backs
With RST, cut 2 Linings

center front seam

decorative stitching lines

With RST, cut 2 Linings
With RST, cut 2 Fronts
Sprout Pants Front
Andy Overalls or Little

pleat

pleat

53

Little Sprouts Baby Pants

Supplies Needed

Fabric:
- for lining, ⅔ yard (6M–18M), ⅞ yard (2T–4T)
- for pants, ¾ yard (6M–18M), 1 yard (2T–4T)

Notions:
- ⅛ yard lightweight fusible interfacing
- ½ yard ⅝"-wide elastic

Sizes: 6M–4T

Cutting & Preparation

1. **Pants Front:** Cut 2 Pants Fronts on page 53, following Enlarging Patterns from a Grid on page 6. Do this again for lining.
2. **Pants Back:** Cut 2 Pants Backs on page 53. Do this again for lining.
3. **Pockets:** Cut 2 Back Pockets on page 52.
4. **Pants Front Waistband:** Cut 1 Pants Front Waistband on page 52.

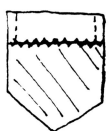

Diagram A

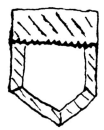

Diagram B

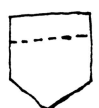

Diagram C

Construction

1. **Pocket:** Finish upper edge of pockets with zigzag stitch. Turn upper edge of pocket tops to outside along fold line as shown in Diagram A. Sew ends and trim. Turn upper edge of pocket to inside as shown in Diagram B. Turn in seam allowance on pocket sides and lower edges and press. On outside, topstitch top of pocket as shown in Diagram C. Pin pockets on pants backs. Edge-stitch in place.

Idea: It is fun to appliqué a vegetable on right back pocket before you sew on pocket.

2. **Pants:** With RST, sew pants fronts together at center front seam. Trim seam below extension and press to left side. Topstitch extension on stitching line as shown on pattern. With RST, sew pants backs together at center back seam. Trim and press to one side.

3. With RST, sew pants back to pants front at side seams. Trim and press seams to one side. Taking a ⅝" seam, sew inner leg seams, trim, and press.

4. Trim off extension on lining and finish lining same as pants. With WST, insert lining into pants, matching seams. Baste top edges together. Pin, then baste front pleats in place.

Diagram D

5. With RST, join front and back waistband at side seams as shown in Diagram D. Trim and press seams open.

6. With WST, fold waistband in half and press to mark top edge of band. Cut a 2½" x 6" piece of interfacing and fuse to wrong side of center front waistband. Press under ½" on one interfaced edge of waistband.

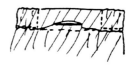

Diagram E

7. Pin right side of unpressed edge of band to lining side of pants, matching side seams. Sew in place. Trim seam and press toward waistband.

8. Fold pressed edge over seam and pin in place. Leaving front section open, topstitch along lower edge of waistband, starting and ending at pleats as shown in Diagram E.

9. Topstitch close to top edge of waistband.

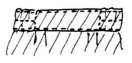

Diagram F

10. Cut elastic to a comfortable waist measurement for your child and insert into waistband. Adjust length and sew ends of elastic in place as shown in Diagram F. Finish sewing across lower front waist-band section.

11. Sew through center of elastic as shown in Diagram G.

Diagram G

12. To hem legs, turn pants and lining edges under ½". Press and sew along bottom edge as shown in Diagram H. Turn up cuff.

Diagram H

Classic Annie Jumper

Sizes: 6M–4T

Cutting & Preparation

1. Cut all Annie Jumper pattern pieces on page 60 for bodice and lining, following Enlarging Patterns from a Grid on page 6.

2. **Interfacing:** (optional) If you are using a lightweight fabric, you may want to interface the front and back bodice pieces. It helps make it more stable. It is not necessary to interface denim or corduroy.

3. **Skirt:** Refer to dimensions below. Cut skirt front, skirt back, and 2 lower skirt bands.

Dimensions for skirt front and skirt back

> 8½" x 24" (6M)
> 9½" x 25" (12M)
> 10½" x 26" (18M)
> 11½" x 27" (2T)
> 12½" x 29" (3T)
> 14" x 30" (4T)

Dimensions for lower skirt band

> 4¼" x 24" (6M)
> 4¼" x 25" (12M)
> 4¼" x 26" (18M)
> 4½" x 27" (2T)
> 4½" x 29" (3T)
> 4½" x 30" (4T)

4. **Pockets:** Cut (8) 2¾" contrasting squares and cut (2) 2" x 5⅛" strips for pocket top. Fold each strip in half lengthwise and press.

Make a cute and classic fashion statement with this sweet patchwork Annie jumper.

Supplies Needed

Fabric:

- for appliqués, assorted scraps
- for bodice lining, ½ yard (6M–18M), ⅝ yard (2T–4T)
- for lower skirt band, ⅓ yard (all sizes)
- for jumper, ¾ yard (6M–18M), ⅞ yard (2T–4T)

Notions:

- (2) 1" buttons
- 1 yard lightweight fusible interfacing (optional)
- ¼ yard lightweight fusible webbing
- fine-tip permanent black pen or dark brown embroidery floss

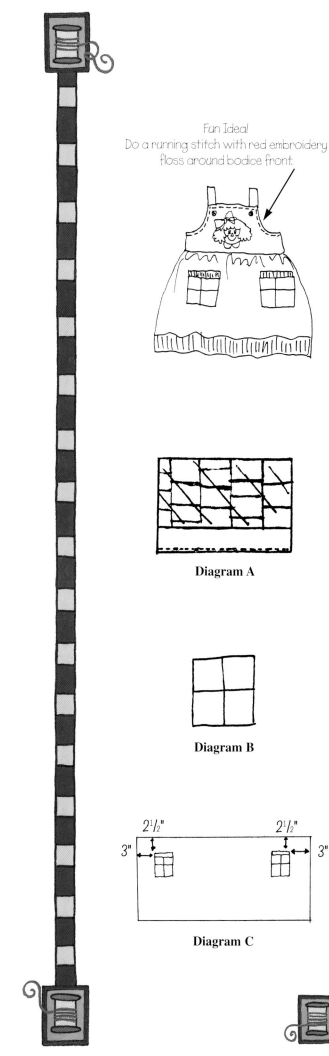

Fun Idea!
Do a running stitch with red embroidery floss around bodice front.

Diagram A

Diagram B

2½"   2½"

3"   3"

Diagram C

Construction

1. **Bodice:** With RST, sew bodice front to bodice back at sides. Do this again for bodice lining. Press seams open.

2. With RST, pin lining to upper edge of bodice front and straps, matching side seams and having raw edges even. Sew, trim corners, and clip curves. Clip seam allowance to stitching at center back. Turn right side out and press. Topstitch edges as you desire. Turn under seam allowance at lower edge of bodice lining and press.

3. **Skirt:** With RST, sew skirt front to skirt back at side seams. With RST, sew lower skirt band at side seams. Press seams open. With WST, fold lower skirt band in half lengthwise and press. With RST, pin and sew raw edges of lower skirt band to bottom of skirt, matching side seams as shown in Diagram A, forming finished hem. Trim and finish seam. Press seam toward skirt.

4. To gather upper edge of skirt, baste ½" and ¼" from raw edge of skirt top. Pull basting to adjust skirt to fit bodice. With RST, pin lower edge of bodice to gathered edge of skirt, matching side seams and leaving bodice lining free. Sew and press seam toward bodice. Sew lining closed over seam with a whipstitch.

5. **Pockets:** With RST, sew (4) 2¾" squares together to make a 4-patch block as shown in Diagram B. Do this again. With RST, sew 2" x 5⅛" pocket top to top edge of 4-patch block. Do this again. Press seams toward 4-patch block. Topstitch pockets onto skirt as shown in Diagram C.

Appliqués

1. Trace and cut Annie from Appliqué Patterns on page 97 as you desire, following General Appliqué Instructions on pages 6–7.
2. Using permanent pen, transfer facial features onto Annie's face. For nose, fuse a triangle of fabric to face with fusible webbing. To add color, use a cotton swab to apply blush on her cheeks.
3. After facial features have been transferred, center appliqué on bodice front as shown in photo on page 56. Fuse appliqué in place. Center fabric triangle on bodice back. Fuse triangle in place.
4. Machine-appliqué around shapes.
5. Tear a 1½" x 13" strip of fabric for Annie's bow. Tie bow and trim ends to desired length. Tack bow in place.

Finishing

1. Make buttonholes in bib as shown in Diagram D.
2. Attach buttons to straps.

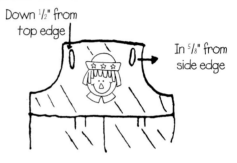

Down ½" from top edge

In ⅝" from side edge

Diagram D

Classic Andy Overalls

Sizes: 6M–4T

Cutting & Preparation

1. Cut all Andy Overalls pattern pieces on pages 53 and 60 for overalls and lining, following Enlarging Patterns from a Grid on page 6. It is not necessary to line pockets.
2. **Interfacing:** (optional) If you are using a lightweight fabric, you may want to interface your front and back bodice pieces. It helps make it more stable. It is not necessary to interface denim or corduroy.

Supplies Needed

Fabric:
- for appliqués, assorted scraps
- for lining, 1⅛ yards (6M–18M), 1⅓ yards (2T–4T)
- for overalls, 1⅛ yards (6M–18M), 1⅓ yards (2T–4T)

Notions:
- (2) 1" button
- 1 yard lightweight fusible interfacing (optional)
- ¼ yard lightweight fusible webbing
- 8 snaps (6M–18M), 10 snaps (2T–4T)

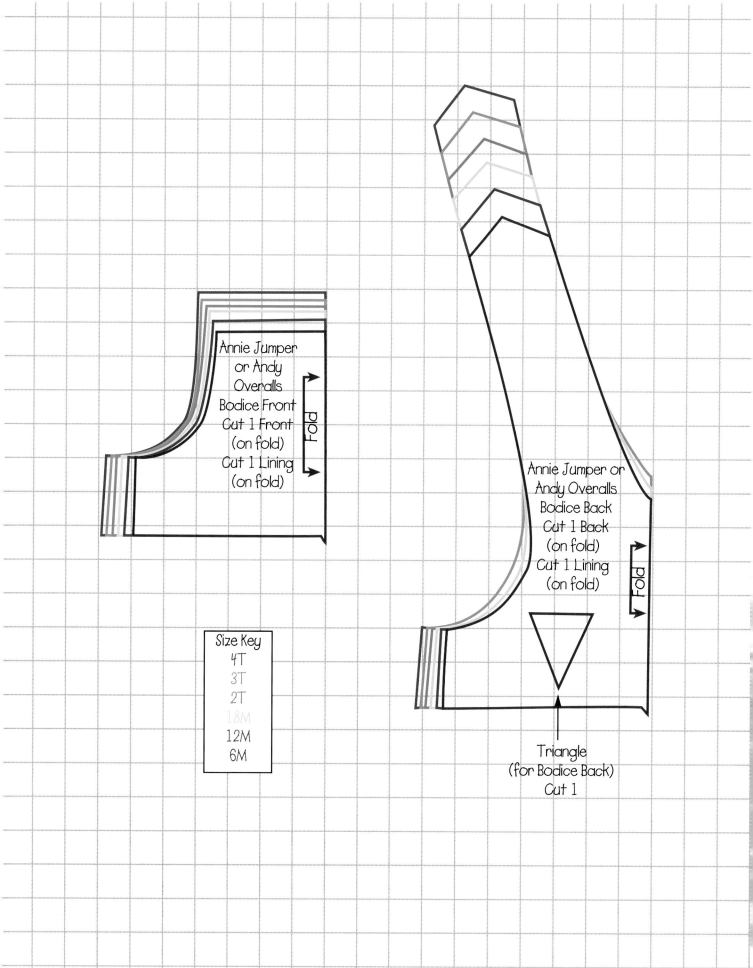

Annie Jumper
or Andy
Overalls
Bodice Front
Cut 1 Front
(on fold)
Cut 1 Lining
(on fold)

Fold

Annie Jumper or
Andy Overalls
Bodice Back
Cut 1 Back
(on fold)
Cut 1 Lining
(on fold)

Fold

Size Key
4T
3T
2T
18M
12M
6M

Triangle
(for Bodice Back)
Cut 1

Construction

1. **Bodice:** With RST, sew bodice front to bodice back at sides. Do this again for bodice lining. Press seams open.

2. With RST, pin lining to upper edge of bodice front and straps, matching side seams and having raw edges even. Sew, trim corners, and clip curves. Clip seam allowance to stitching at center back as shown in Diagram A. Turn right side out and press. Topstitch edges as you desire. Turn under seam allowance at lower edge of bodice lining and press.

3. **Pockets:** Finish upper edge of pockets with zigzag stitch. Turn upper edge of pocket tops to right side along fold line as shown in Diagram B. Sew ends and trim. Turn upper edge of pocket to inside as shown in Diagram C. Turn in seam allowance on pocket sides and lower edges and press. On outside, topstitch top of pocket as shown in Diagram D. Pin pockets on back of pants as shown in Diagram E. Topstitch in place.

4. **Pants:** With RST, sew front pants sections together at center front seam. Trim seam below extension and press to left side. Topstitch extension on stitching line as shown on Overalls Pattern. With RST, sew pant backs together at center back seam. Trim seam and press to one side.

5. With RST, sew pants back to pants front at side seams. Trim seams to ¼" and press to one side. Trim off front extensions on lining. Finish lining same as pants. Trim seams to ¼" and press to one side. With RST, pin pant inner leg edges together

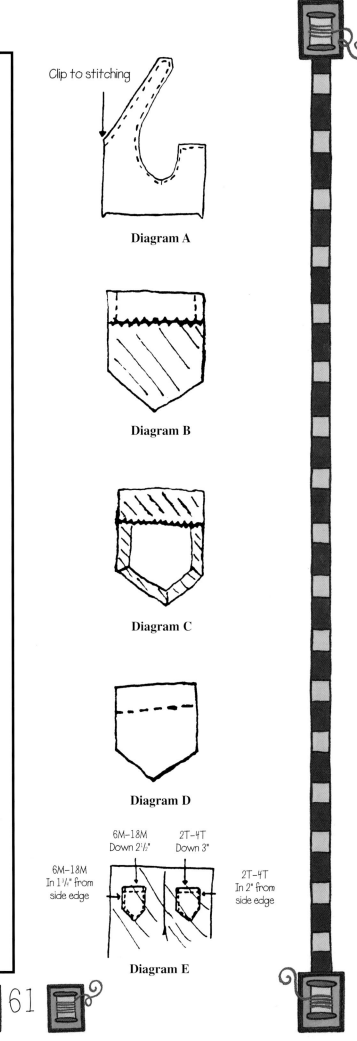

Clip to stitching

Diagram A

Diagram B

Diagram C

Diagram D

6M–18M
Down 2½"

2T–4T
Down 3"

6M–18M
In 1¾" from side edge

2T–4T
In 2" from side edge

Diagram E

with lining, matching seams with raw edges even. Taking a ⅜" seam allowance, sew as shown in Diagram F. Trim seams and corners. Turn to right side and press. Sew along edge of leg and crotch, then sew ½" from first row of stitching.

6. With RST, pin and baste top edges of pants and lining together, matching side seams. Pin pleats in pants front and baste in place.

7. With RST, pin bodice to pants top, matching side seams and center front notch to center front seam, being careful to keep bodice lining free. Sew in place and press seam toward bodice. Sew lining closed over seam with a whipstitch.

Note: If making overalls without snaps in crotch, follow Construction for Little Sprouts Baby Pants on pages 54–55.

Appliqués

1. Trace and cut Andy from Appliqué Patterns on page 97 as you desire, following General Appliqué Instructions on pages 6–7.

2. Using permanent pen, transfer facial features onto Andy's face. For nose, fuse a triangle of fabric to face with fusible webbing. To add color, use a cotton swab to apply blush on his cheeks.

3. After facial features have been transferred, center appliqué on bodice front as shown in photo on page 56. Fuse appliqué in place. Center fabric triangle on bodice back. Fuse triangle in place.

4. Machine-appliqué around shapes.

Finishing

1. Make buttonholes in bib as shown in Diagram G.

2. Attach buttons to straps.

3. Evenly space snaps and attach them along crotch.

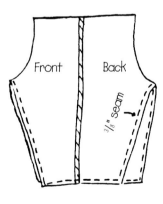

Front   Back

⅜" seam

Diagram F

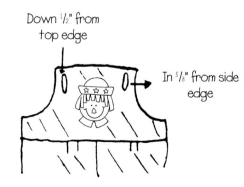

Down ½" from top edge

In ⅝" from side edge

Diagram G

Loose Threads Patch Vest

Supplies Needed

Fabric:

- for front, ½ yard flannel (kids' 4–5),
  ¾ yard flannel (kids' 6–14),
  ¾ yard flannel (women's 6–18),
  1 yard flannel (women's 20–24)
- for back and lining, 1 yard (kids'
  4–5), 1¼ yards (kids' 6–8),
  1⅜ yards (kids' 10–14), 2¼ yards
  (women's all sizes)
- for piecing vest fronts and
  appliqués, assorted scraps

Notions:

- ¼ yard lightweight fusible webbing
  (kids'), ½ yard lightweight fusible
  webbing (women's)
- for appliqués, coordinating thread
- for vest front and vest ties, (5)
  ⅝" buttons (kids'), (5) 1" buttons
  (women's)
- for all fabrics, neutral-colored
  thread

Sizes: kids' 4–14, women's 6–16

Cutting & Preparation

1. **Vest Fronts:** Cut 2 Vest Fronts on page 67
   or 68 from unwashed flannel, following
   Enlarging Patterns from a Grid on page 6.
   Do this again for lining. Cut assorted sizes
   of squares and rectangles from scraps.

   *Note: General guidelines for squares and
   rectangles are shown on patterns for an
   organized look. If choosing to use these
   guides, add ⅛" to all sides of squares and
   rectangles before cutting fabric, so when
   squares and rectangles are laid on the flannel
   they will cover it completely.*

2. Lay assorted rectangles on vest fronts,
   overlapping slightly to cover flannel
   completely. Starting in center of vest, pin
   each rectangle securely to flannel. Trim off
   any excess fabric around outside edges of
   vest fronts. Beginning in center of vest,
   sew closely around edges of each
   rectangle.

3. **Vest Back:** Cut 1 Vest Back on page 67 or
   69. Do this again for lining.

4. Baste around outside edges of both vest
   fronts as shown in Diagram A.

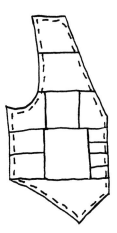

Diagram A

Construction

1. With RST, pin vest front to vest back at shoulder seams and sew as shown in Diagram B. Press seam open. Do this again for vest lining.

2. Press under seam allowance on side seams of front and back lining. With RST, pin vest to vest lining and sew, leaving side seams open. Trim seams and corners. Clip curves. Turn right side out through one side opening and press.

3. With RST, pin side seams together and sew as shown in Diagram C. Be careful not to catch lining. Trim and press seam open. Sew lining closed over seam with a whipstitch.

4. Crazy-stitch over vest fronts, following General Sewing Instructions on pages 8–9. Cover all areas so that lining and flannel are securely attached to vest front. Wash and dry vest (in dryer). This will slightly shrink and "age" the vest.

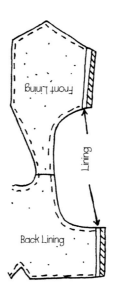

Diagram B

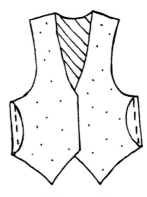

Diagram C

Appliqués

1. Trace and cut Garden Patch shapes from Appliqué Patterns on pages 118–123 for vest as you desire, following General Appliqué Instructions on pages 6–7.

2. Fuse appliqués onto vest with fusible webbing. For vest back, appliqué back tab with three stars as shown in Diagram D. For women's vest, place tab 2" from center neck edge. For kids' vest, place tab 1" from center neck edge.

3. Machine-appliqué around all pieces.

Diagram D

Diagram E

Finishing

1. Topstitch ¼" all around vest and armholes.

2. Fold all edges of each vest tie under ¼" and press to form a crease. With WST, fold tie in half lengthwise. Sew along all folded edges as shown in Diagram E. Sew ties onto vest back, following Vest Back pattern on page 67 or 69 for placement.

3. Sew 2 buttons over edges of vest ties as shown in Diagram D on page 65. Tie knot in vest ties.

4. Make 3 buttonholes on right vest front for girls and women or left vest front for boys. Sew on buttons.

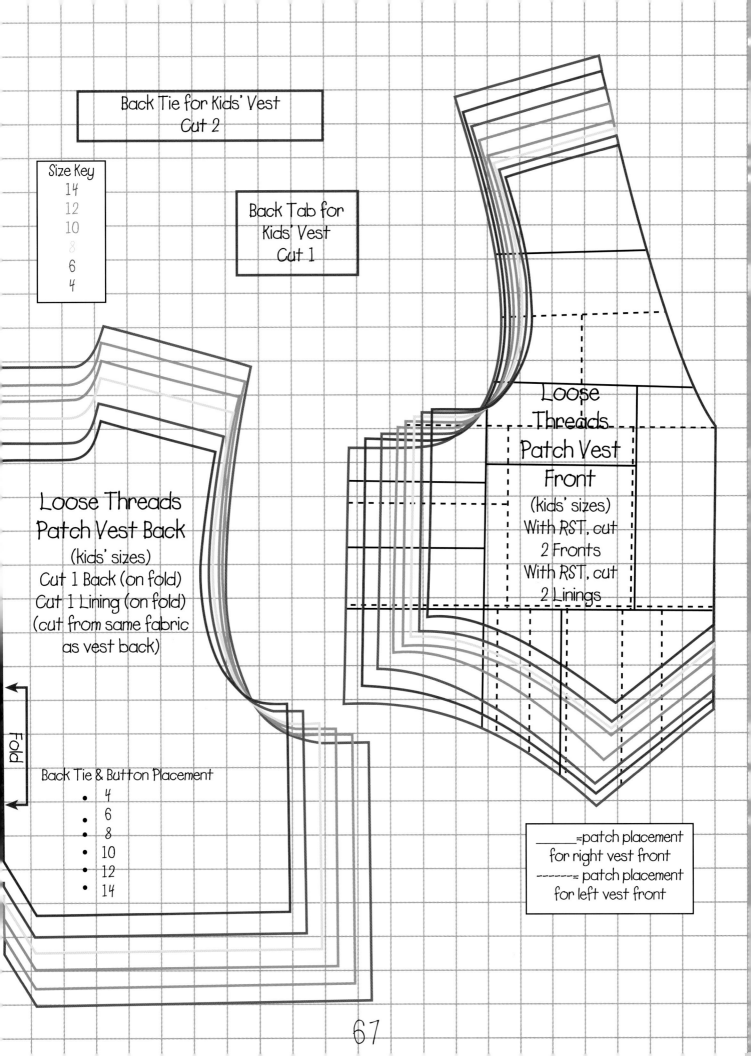

Back Tie for Kids' Vest
Cut 2

Size Key
14
12
10
8
6
4

Back Tab for
Kids' Vest
Cut 1

Loose Threads
Patch Vest Back

(kids' sizes)
Cut 1 Back (on fold)
Cut 1 Lining (on fold)
(cut from same fabric
as vest back)

Fold

Back Tie & Button Placement
• 4
• 6
• 8
• 10
• 12
• 14

Loose
Threads
Patch Vest
Front
(kids' sizes)
With RST, cut
2 Fronts
With RST, cut
2 Linings

_____=patch placement
for right vest front
- - - - - - = patch placement
for left vest front

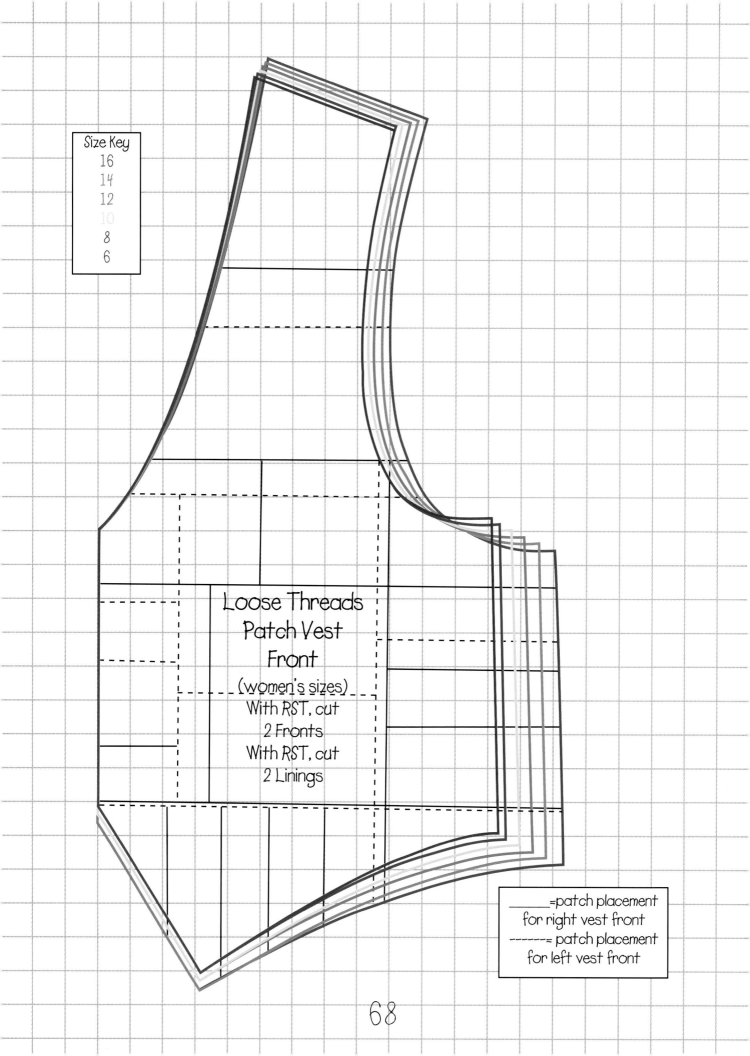

Size Key
16
14
12
10
8
6

Loose Threads
Patch Vest
Front
(women's sizes)
With RST, cut
2 Fronts
With RST, cut
2 Linings

_____=patch placement
for right vest front
-------= patch placement
for left vest front

68

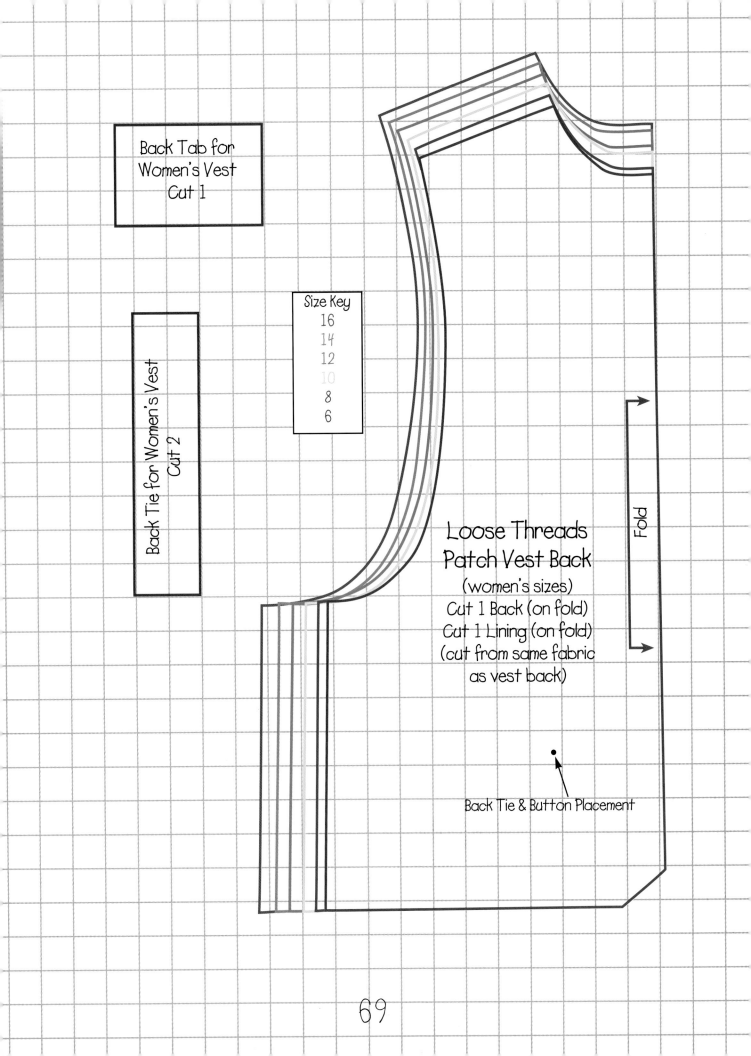

Back Tab for
Women's Vest
Cut 1

Back Tie for Women's Vest
Cut 2

Size Key
16
14
12
10
8
6

Loose Threads
Patch Vest Back
(women's sizes)
Cut 1 Back (on fold)
Cut 1 Lining (on fold)
(cut from same fabric
as vest back)

Fold

Back Tie & Button Placement

69

Garden Patch Jumpers

Sizes: kids' 2–14, women's 6–14

Supplies Needed

Fabric:

- for appliqués, assorted scraps
- for bodice front and back, ¼ yard (kids' 2–6), ⅓ yard (kids' 8–14), ⅜ yard (women's 6–12), ⅞ yard (women's 14)
- for bodice lining, ¼ yard (kids' 2–6), ⅓ yard (kids' 8–14), ⅜ yard (women's 6–12), ⅞ yard (women's 14)
- for lower skirt band, ⅜ yard fabric (kids' 2–5), ½ yard (kids' 6–14 and women's 6–12), ⅔ yard (women's 14)
- for skirt, assorted ⅛–½ yard of each fabric as shown in appropriate Skirt Cutting Diagrams on page 72
- for strap facings, ½ yard (for all sizes)

Notions:

- ½ yard lightweight fusible webbing
- (4) 1" buttons (kids'), (4) 1¼" buttons (women's)
- for appliqués, neutral-colored thread embroidery floss (optional)
- for crow jumper, 2 black beads or round buttons
- for straps ½ yard regular fusible interfacing (optional)

Cutting & Preparation

1. Cut all Garden Patch Jumper pattern pieces on page 75 as you desire, following Enlarging Patterns from a Grid on page 6. For patchwork straps, cut out 6–7 squares of fabric for each strap (all sizes). With RST, sew squares into a strip before cutting straps from pattern as shown in Diagram A. Cut strap facings from one piece of fabric. Cut straps from fusible interfacing as you desire.

2. **Interfacing:** (optional) If you are using a lightweight fabric, you may want to interface the front and back bodice pieces. It helps to make it more stable. It is not necessary to interface denim or corduroy.

3. **Skirt:** Cut assorted patches for skirt, following appropriate Skirt Cutting Diagrams on page 72.

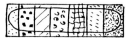

Diagram A

Skirt Cutting Diagrams

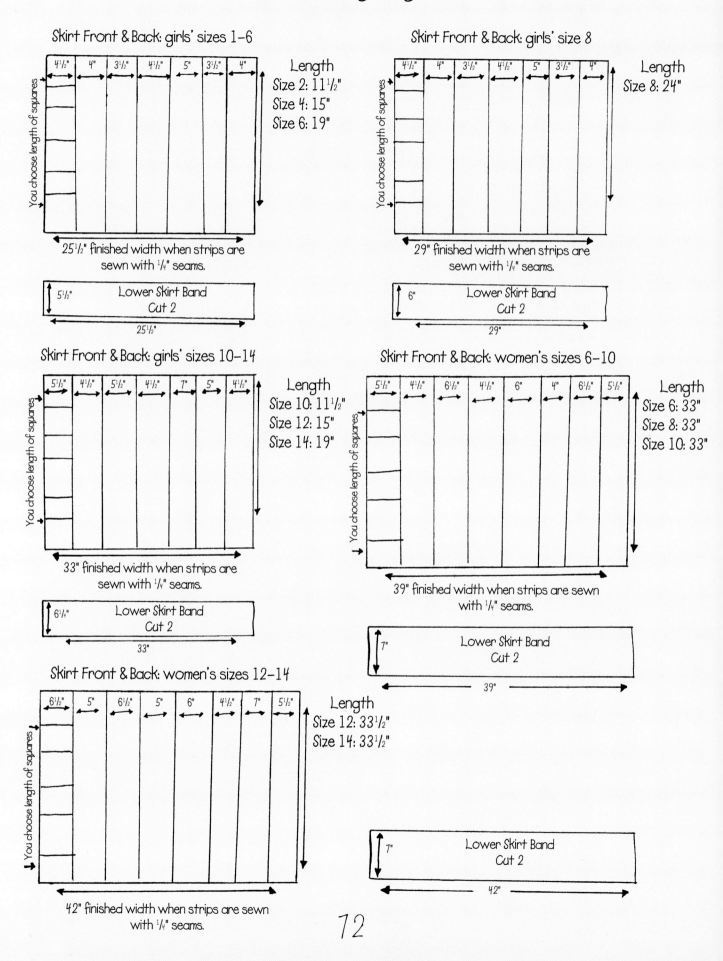

Skirt Front & Back: girls' sizes 1–6

4¹/₂" 4" 3¹/₂" 4¹/₂" 5" 3¹/₂" 4"

You choose length of squares

Length
Size 2: 11¹/₂"
Size 4: 15"
Size 6: 19"

25¹/₂" finished width when strips are sewn with ¹/₄" seams.

5¹/₂" | Lower Skirt Band Cut 2
25¹/₂"

Skirt Front & Back: girls' size 8

4¹/₂" 4" 3¹/₂" 4¹/₂" 5" 3¹/₂" 4"

You choose length of squares

Length
Size 8: 24"

29" finished width when strips are sewn with ¹/₄" seams.

6" | Lower Skirt Band Cut 2
29"

Skirt Front & Back: girls' sizes 10–14

5¹/₂" 4¹/₂" 5¹/₂" 4¹/₂" 7" 5" 4¹/₂"

You choose length of squares

Length
Size 10: 11¹/₂"
Size 12: 15"
Size 14: 19"

33" finished width when strips are sewn with ¹/₄" seams.

6¹/₄" | Lower Skirt Band Cut 2
33"

Skirt Front & Back: women's sizes 6–10

5¹/₂" 4¹/₂" 6¹/₂" 4¹/₂" 6" 4" 6¹/₂" 5¹/₂"

You choose length of squares

Length
Size 6: 33"
Size 8: 33"
Size 10: 33"

39" finished width when strips are sewn with ¹/₄" seams.

7" | Lower Skirt Band Cut 2
39"

Skirt Front & Back: women's sizes 12–14

6¹/₂" 5" 6¹/₂" 5" 6" 4¹/₂" 7" 5¹/₂"

You choose length of squares

Length
Size 12: 33¹/₂"
Size 14: 33¹/₂"

42" finished width when strips are sewn with ¹/₄" seams.

7" | Lower Skirt Band Cut 2
42"

72

Appliqués

1. Trace and cut Garden Patch shapes (including background blocks) from Appliqué Patterns on pages 118–123 as you desire, following General Appliqué Instructions on pages 6–7.

2. For watering can jumper, cut (2) 1" x 6½" strips and (2) 1" x 8" strips. With RST, sew 1" x 6½" strips to sides of background block. With RST, sew 1" x 8" strips to top and bottom of background block. Press seams toward stripping.

3. Center and fuse appliqués onto background block with fusible webbing. Center and fuse background block onto bodice front.

4. Machine-appliqué around shape and background block.

5. For crow jumper, sew black beads on crow for eyes.

Construction

1. **Bodice:** With RST, sew bodice front to bodice back at side seams. Do this again for bodice lining. Press seams open.

2. With RST, pin lining to upper edge of bodice front, matching side seams and having raw edges even as shown in Diagram B. Sew, trim seams, clip corners, turn right side out, and press. Turn under seam allowance at lower edge of lining ⅝" and press.

3. **Optional:** Topstitch upper edges and sides of bodice front and back with contrasting color embroidery floss with a running stitch as shown in Diagram C,

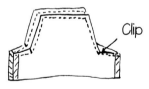

Diagram B

optional running stitch

Diagram C

following General Embroidery Instructions on page 7.

4. Fuse interfacing onto wrong side of strap facing. With RST, pin strap facing to pieced strap. Taking a ¼" seam, sew around strap, leaving an opening for turning. Trim seams and clip curves. Turn right side out and press. Hand-stitch opening closed.

5. Taking ¼" seam and with RST, sew patches to dimensions for skirt front and back as shown in appropriate Skirt Cutting Diagrams on page 72. Fuse appliqués onto skirt as you desire as shown in photos on pages 70–73.

Note: The length for the women's jumper is designed to go 2" above the ankle of a 5' 5" person. If you are shorter or taller than this, make the necessary adjustments in skirt length.

6. **Pockets:** Mark circles on front and back of skirt as shown in Diagram D. Taking ¼" seam allowance and with RST, sew one pocket to each side edge of skirt front and skirt back as shown in Diagram E. Press seam toward pocket and press pocket away from skirt.

7. **Skirt:** With RST, pin skirt front to skirt back at sides, matching pockets. Sew from upper edge of skirt to circle as shown in Diagram F. Sew around pocket, pivoting where pocket meets skirt and continue sewing down skirt side seam. Trim, finish, and press seams toward skirt front.

8. To gather upper edge of skirt, baste ⅜" and ⅝" from raw edge of skirt top, breaking basting at side seams and keeping pockets free.

9. With RST, sew lower skirt band at side seams. Press seams open. With WST, fold lower skirt band in half lengthwise and press. With RST, pin and sew raw edge of lower skirt band to bottom of skirt, matching side seams as shown in Diagram G, forming finished hem. Trim and finish seam. Press seam toward skirt.

10. Make a buttonhole on one end of each strap as shown in Diagram H. Make buttonholes on bodice back as shown in Diagram I.

11. With RST pin lower edge of bodice front and back to upper edge of skirt, matching skirt side seams to bodice side seams. Pull basting and adjust gathers evenly to fit. Pin pockets towards skirt front and catch them in the seam. Sew, taking a ⅝" seam. Trim seam and press toward bodice. Sew lining closed over seam with a whipstitch.

12. Sew buttons on bodice front. Try on jumper. Mark button placement on end of strap opposite buttonhole. Sew remaining buttons on straps.

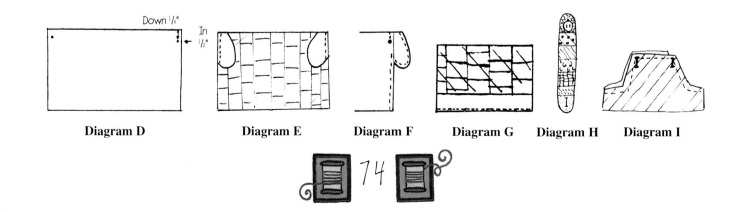

Diagram D   **Diagram E**   **Diagram F**   **Diagram G**   **Diagram H**   **Diagram I**

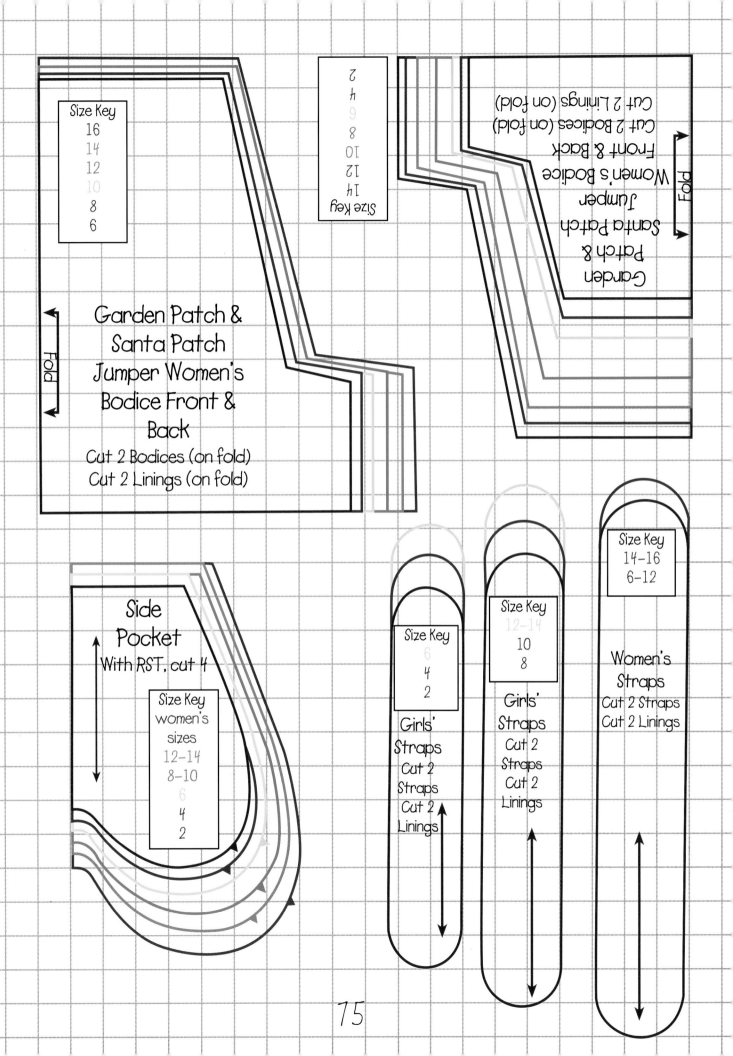

Size Key
16
14
12
10
8
6

Garden Patch &
Santa Patch
Jumper Women's
Bodice Front &
Back
Cut 2 Bodices (on fold)
Cut 2 Linings (on fold)

Fold

Size Key
14
12
10
8
6
4
2

Garden Patch &
Santa Patch
Jumper
Women's Bodice
Front & Back
Cut 2 Bodices (on fold)
Cut 2 Linings (on fold)

Fold

Side
Pocket
With RST, cut 4

Size Key
women's
sizes
12-14
8-10
6
4
2

Size Key
6
4
2

Girls'
Straps
Cut 2
Straps
Cut 2
Linings

Size Key
12-14
10
8

Girls'
Straps
Cut 2
Straps
Cut 2
Linings

Size Key
14-16
6-12

Women's
Straps
Cut 2 Straps
Cut 2 Linings

75

Santa Patch Jumper

Add some jolly joy to your holidays by stitching up one of these merry jumpers.

Supplies Needed

Fabric:
- for appliqués, assorted scraps
- for bodice front and back, ¼ yard (kids' 1–6), ⅓ yard (kids' 8–14), ⅜ yard (women's 6–12), ⅞ yard (women's 14–24)
- for bodice lining, ¼ yard (kids' 1–6), ⅓ yard (kids' 8–14), ⅜ yard (women's 6–12), ⅞ yard (women's 14–24)
- for lower skirt band, ⅜ yard (kids' 1–5), ½ yard (kids' 6–14 and women's 6–12), ⅔ yard (women's 14–24)
- for skirt, assorted ⅛–½ yards of each fabric as shown in appropriate Skirt Cutting Diagrams on page 72
- for strap facings, ½ yard (for all sizes)

Notions:
- ½ yard lightweight fusible webbing
- (4) 1" buttons (kids')
- (4) 1¼" buttons (women's)
- for appliqués, neutral-colored thread
- black embroidery floss
- for straps, ½ yard regular fusible interfacing (optional)

Sizes: kids' 1–14, women's 6–24

Cutting & Preparation

1. Cut all Garden Patch Jumper pattern pieces on page 75 as you desire, following Enlarging Patterns from a Grid on page 6. For patchwork straps, cut out 6–7 squares of fabric for each strap (all sizes). With RST, sew squares into a strip before cutting straps from pattern as shown in Diagram A on page 79. Cut strap facings from one piece of fabric. Cut straps from fusible interfacing as you desire.

2. **Interfacing:** (optional) If you are using a lightweight fabric, you may want to interface the front and back bodice pieces. It helps to make it more stable. It is not necessary to interface denim or corduroy.

3. **Skirt:** Cut assorted patches for skirt, following appropriate Skirt Cutting Diagrams on page 72.

Appliqués

1. Trace and cut Santa shape from Appliqué Patterns on page 124 as you desire, following General Appliqué Instructions on pages 6–7. Cut background block the width of Santa's coat.

2. Cut (4) 1¼" x 8½" strips for kids' bodice and (4) 1½" x 10" strips for women's bodice as shown in photo on page 77. With RST, sew strips to sides of background block. Trim excess. With RST, sew

remaining strips to top and bottom of background block. Press seams toward stripping.

3. Center and fuse appliqués onto background block with fusible webbing. Center and fuse background block onto bodice front.

4. Blanket stitch around shape and background block, following General Embroidery Instructions on page 7.

5. To make Santa's nose, stuff a small piece of batting in a small scrap of fabric as shown in Diagram B. Form nose shape in center of fabric. Tack nose in place. Wind thread around base and secure in place, leaving needle and thread attached. Trim raw edge of fabric close to thread. Stitch nose onto Santa face, tucking raw edges under nose. Knot thread to secure and cut.

6. To add color, use a cotton swab to apply blush on his cheeks.

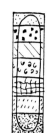

Diagram A   **Diagram B**

Construction

1. **Bodice:** With RST, sew bodice front to bodice back at side seams. Do this again for bodice lining. Press seams open.

2. With RST, pin lining to upper edge of bodice front, matching side seams and having raw edges even as shown in Diagram C. Sew, trim seams, clip corners, turn right side out, and press. Turn under seam allowance at lower edge of lining ⅝" and press.

3. **Optional:** Sew upper edges and sides of bodice front and back with contrasting color embroidery floss with a running

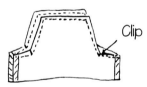

Clip

Diagram C

optional
running stitch

Diagram D

stitch as shown in Diagram D on page 79 following General Embroidery Instructions on page 7.

4. Fuse interfacing onto wrong side of strap facing. With RST, pin strap facing to pieced strap. Taking a ¼" seam, sew around strap, leaving an opening for turning. Trim seams and clip curves. Turn right side out and press. Hand-stitch opening closed.

5. Taking ¼" seam and with RST, sew patches to dimensions for skirt front and back as shown in appropriate Skirt Cutting Diagrams on page 72.

Note: The length for the women's jumper is designed to go 2" above the ankle of a 5' 5" person. If you are shorter or taller than this, make the necessary adjustments on skirt length.

6. **Pockets:** Mark circles on front and back of skirt as shown in Diagram E. Taking ¼" seam allowance and with RST, sew one pocket to each side edge of skirt front and skirt back as shown in Diagram F. Press seam toward pocket and press pocket away from skirt.

7. **Skirt:** With RST, pin skirt front to skirt back at sides, matching pockets. Sew from upper edge of skirt to circle as shown in Diagram G. Sew around pocket, pivoting where pocket meets skirt and continue sewing down skirt side seam. Trim, finish, and press seams toward skirt front.

8. To gather upper edge of skirt, baste ⅜" and ⅝" from raw edge of skirt top, ending basting at side seams and keeping pockets free.

9. With RST, sew lower skirt band at side seams. Press seams open. With WST, fold lower skirt band in half lengthwise and press. With RST, pin and sew raw edge of lower skirt band to bottom of skirt, matching side seams as shown in Diagram H, forming finished hem. Trim and finish seam. Press seam toward skirt.

10. Make a buttonhole on one end of each strap as shown in Diagram I. Make buttonholes on bodice back as shown in Diagram J.

11. With RST, pin lower edge of bodice front and back to upper edge of skirt, matching skirt side seams to bodice side seams. Pull basting and adjust gathers evenly to fit. Pin pockets towards skirt front and catch them in the seam. Sew, taking a ⅝" seam. Trim seam and press toward bodice. Sew lining closed over seam with a whipstitch.

12. Sew buttons on bodice front. Try on jumper. Mark button placement on end of strap opposite buttonhole. Sew remaining buttons on straps.

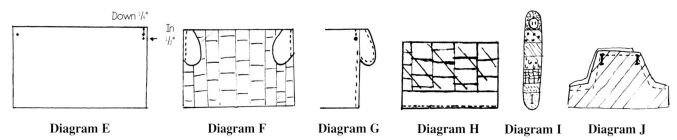

Diagram E   Diagram F   Diagram G   Diagram H   Diagram I   Diagram J

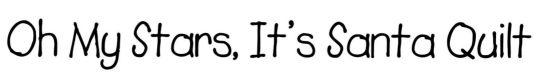

Oh My Stars, It's Santa Quilt

Santa feels very friendly in this colorful and festive wall quilt. Have fun with this merry old fellow as you create a darling quilt to add sparkle to your home for the holidays.

Supplies Needed

Batting:
• 36" x 45"

Fabric:
• for 1st border, ¼ yard
• for 2nd border and star block, ½ yard gold
• for 3rd border, ½ yard
• for appliqués and star centers, assorted scraps
• for backing, 1 yard
• for binding, ⅓ yard
• for Santa background, ¼ yard light-colored
• for star block, ¼ yard green

Notions:
• ¼ yard lightweight fusible webbing
• 5 small jingle bells
• black embroidery floss
• fine-tip permanent black pen

Finished size 27" x 27"

Cutting & Preparation

1. **Santa Blocks:** Cut (5) 6½" light-colored background blocks.
2. **1st Border:** Cut (2) 1½" x 18½" strips for top and bottom of quilt top and (2) 1½" x 20½" strips for sides of quilt top.
3. **2nd Border:** Cut (2) 1" x 20½" strips for top and bottom of quilt top and (2) 1" x 21½" strips for sides of quilt top.
4. **3rd Border:** Cut (2) 3¼" x 21½" strips for top and bottom of quilt top and (2) 3¼" x 27" strips for sides of quilt top.
5. **Binding:** Cut (3) 2½" x 45" strips.
6. **Pieced Star Blocks:** Cut 36 of Template 1 on page 84 for 9-patch centers as you desire, 16 green of Template 2 for outside triangles of block, 32 gold of Template 3 for star points, and 16 green of Template 4 for outside corners of block.
7. With RST, piece and sew 4 pieced star blocks as shown in Diagram A.

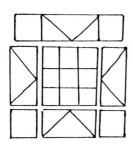

Diagram A

Appliqués

1. Trace and cut 5 Santa shapes from Appliqué Patterns on page 124 as you desire, following General Appliqué Instructions on pages 6–7.
2. Center and fuse 1 appliqué onto each background block with fusible webbing as shown in photo on page 81.

3. Using 2–3 strands of embroidery floss, blanket-stitch around shapes, following General Embroidery Instructions on page 7.

4. Tack a jingle bell to tip of each Santa hat.

5. To make Santa's nose, stuff a small piece of batting in a small scrap of fabric as shown in Diagram B. Form nose shape in center of fabric. Tack nose in place. Wind thread around base and secure in place, leaving needle and thread attached. Trim raw fabric edges close to thread. Stitch nose onto Santa face, tucking raw edges under nose. Knot thread to secure and cut.

6. To add color, use a cotton swab to apply blush on his cheeks.

7. Using black permanent pen, draw Santa's eyes and eyebrows as shown on Santa appliqué pattern on page 124.

Construction

1. With RST, sew Santa and pieced star blocks together to form center of quilt as shown in Diagram C.

2. **1st Border:** With RST, sew 1½" x 18½" strips to top and bottom of quilt top and 1½" x 20½" strips to sides of quilt top.

3. **2nd Border:** With RST, sew 1" x 20½" strips to top and bottom of quilt top and 1" x 21½" strips to sides of quilt top.

4. **3rd Border:** With RST, sew 3¼" x 21½" strips to top and bottom of quilt top and 3¼" x 27" strips to sides of quilt top.

5. Finish quilt, following General Finishing Instructions on page 8.

Diagram B

Diagram C

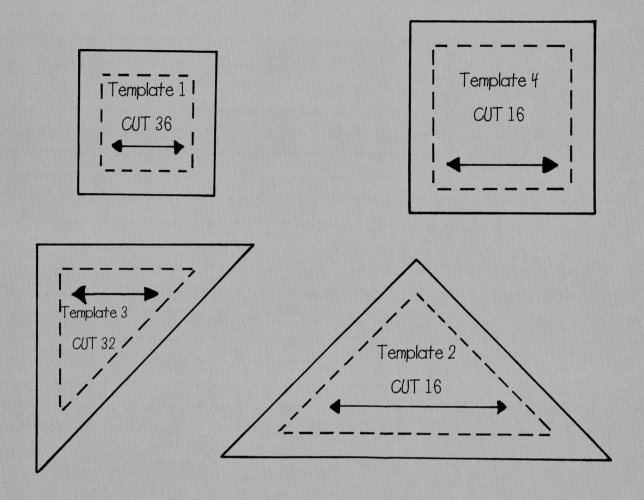

Template 1

CUT 36

Template 4

CUT 16

Template 3

CUT 32

Template 2

CUT 16

"...Peace on earth..."   "...joy to the world..."   "...Glad tidings to all..."

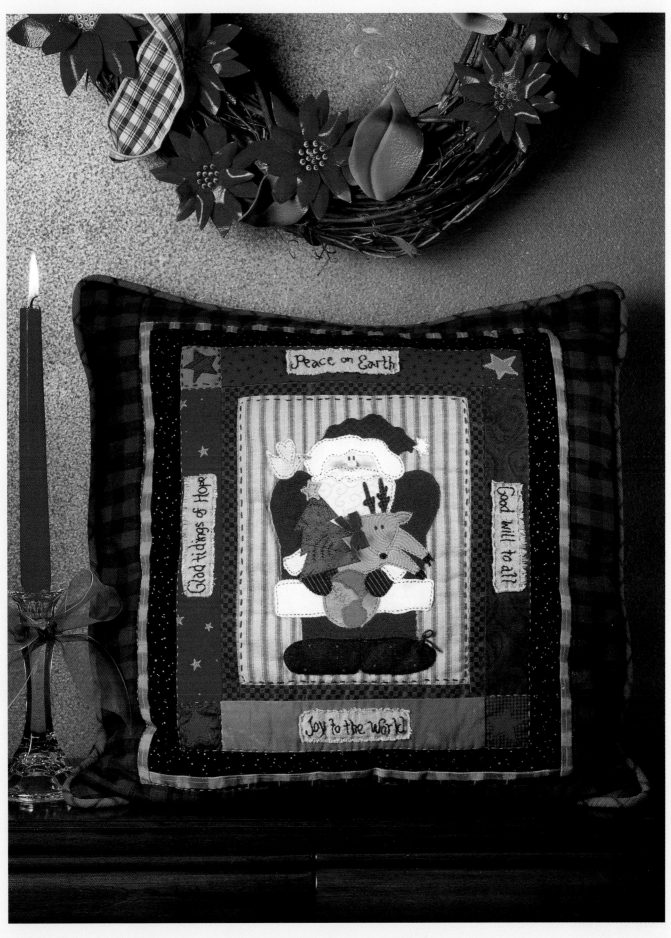

85

Santa Pillow

Add peace to your season and joy to your world as you stitch up this dear Santa pillow for yourself or for someone you love.

Supplies Needed

* 18" pillow form

Batting:
* 23" x 45"

Fabric:
* for background, ⅓ yard
* for backing, ½ yard
* for pillow back, ¾ yard
* for stripping and appliqués, assorted scraps

Notions:
* 1 yard lightweight fusible webbing
* 2¼ yards piping
* black or brown embroidery floss
* fine-tip permanent black pen

Finished size: 18¼" x 18¼"

Cutting & Preparation

Note: There are lots of border pieces to this pillow. It will be helpful if you lay out pieces as shown in Diagram A or photo on page 85 before sewing it together.

1. **Pillow Top:** Cut (1) 7½" x 9¼" background piece.
2. **1st Border:** Cut (2) 1" x 7½" strips for top and bottom and (2) 1" x 10¼" strips for sides.
3. **2nd Border:** Cut (2) 2" x 10¼" assorted strips for sides, (2) 2" x 8½" assorted strips for top and bottom, and (4) 2" assorted squares for corners.
4. **3rd Border:** Cut (2) 1½" x 13¼" strips for sides and (2) 1" x 13½" strips for top and bottom.
5. **4th Border:** Cut (2) 1" x 14¼" strips for sides and (2) 1" x 14½" strips for top and bottom.
6. **5th Border:** Cut (2) 2⅝" x 15¼" strips for sides and (2) 2⅛" x 18¾" strips for top and bottom.
7. **Pillow Back:** Cut (2) 18¾" x 24" pieces.

Diagram A

Appliqués

1. Trace and cut Santa shapes from Appliqué Patterns on page 125, following General Appliqué Instructions on pages 6–7.

2. Fuse appliqués to 7½" x 9¼" background piece with fusible webbing as shown in photo on page 85.

3. Fuse stars to corner squares on 2nd border as shown in photo.

4. Machine-appliqué around all shapes.

5. To make Santa's nose, stuff a small piece of batting in a small scrap of fabric as shown in Diagram B. Form nose shape in center of fabric. Tack nose in place. Wind thread around base and secure, leaving needle and thread attached. Trim raw fabric edges close to thread. Stitch nose onto Santa face, tucking raw edges under nose. Knot thread to secure and cut.

6. To add color, use a cotton swab to apply blush on his cheeks.

7. Pen-stitch around fabric shapes as shown in photo on page 85, following General Pen-stitching Instructions on page 9.

Construction

1. **1st Border:** With RST, sew 1" x 7½" strips to top and bottom of background piece for pillow top as shown in Diagram C. With RST, sew 1" x 10¼" strips to sides of pillow top.

2. **2nd Border:** With RST, sew 2" x 10¼" strips to sides of pillow top. With RST, sew 2" corner squares to ends of 2" x 8½" border strips and sew finished strips to top and bottom of pillow top.

3. **3rd Border:** With RST, sew 1½" x 13¼" strips to sides of pillow top. Sew 1" x 13½" strips to top and bottom of pillow top.

Diagram B

Diagram C

4. **4th Border:** With RST, sew 1" x 14¼" strips to sides of pillow top. With RST, sew 1" x 14½" strips to top and bottom of pillow top.

5. **5th Border:** With RST, sew 2⅝" x 15¼" strips to sides of pillow top. With RST, sew 2⅛" x 18¾" strips to top and bottom of pillow top.

6. **Batting:** Cut a square of backing and a square of batting the same size as pillow top. Layer batting between wrong side of pillow top and backing. Baste through all layers. Quilt around shapes and borders.

7. **Pillow Top:** Tie a fabric bow and tack to reindeer's neck. Using 3 strands of embroidery floss, sew a running stitch ¼" from the edge of background fabric, following General Embroidery Instructions on page 7. Using 4 strands of embroidery floss, embroider holiday greeting on 1½" x 4½" pieces. Trim as you desire and hand-stitch to pillow front with a running stitch. For a more frayed look, rip fabric 1" x 4" and carefully embroider holiday greeting.

8. **Piping:** Pin piping to front side of pillow top with raw edges together. Slightly round corners of pillow top. Clip piping at corners for ease in sewing as shown in Diagram D. Sew as close as possible to cording so existing stitching line does not show on pillow front.

Note: To hand-make piping, see General Sewing Instructions on pages 8–9.

9. **Pillow Back:** Fold (2) 18¾" x 24" pieces of fabric in half, forming (2) 12" x 18¾" pieces. Press to set crease. Overlap folded edges so that pillow back is same size as pillow front. Pin and baste all raw edges together. With RST, pin pillow front to pillow back. Sew in place, following piping stitching line. Clip corners and turn right side out.

10. Insert pillow form.

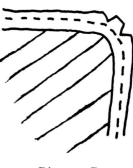

Diagram D

Very Merry Christmas Wall Quilt

This special little quilt is perfect for showing off your holiday spirit and for using up those small leftover pieces of your favorite fabrics.

Supplies Needed

Batting:
• 27" x 45"

Fabric:
• for 1st border, ¼ yard
• for backing, ¾ yard
• for binding, ⅜ yard
• for pieced outside border and quilt top, assorted scraps

Notions:
• ¼ yard regular fusible webbing
• assorted buttons
• fine-tip permanent black pen
• gold glitter glue (optional)

Finished size 24" x 24"

Cutting & Preparation

1. **Background:** Cut (9) 6½" assorted background blocks.
2. Cut (9) 4¾" squares.
3. Cut (9) 3½" squares.
4. **1st Border:** Cut (2) 1¼" x 19" strips for top and bottom of quilt top and (2) 1¼" x 21" strips for sides of quilt top.
5. **Pieced Outside Border:** Cut 1¼"–1¾" x 22" strips. With RST, sew strips together for (1) 13" x 22" strip as shown in Diagram A. From this strip, cut (8) 2½" x 13" strips. With RST, sew (2) 2½" x 13" strips for (1) 2½" x 25½" strip. Do this again for 4 strips as shown in Diagram B.
6. Center and sew 3½" squares onto 4¾" squares with a running stitch, following General Embroidery Instructions on page 7.
7. Center and sew 4¾" squares onto 6½" background blocks with a running stitch.

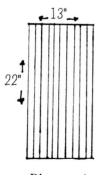

← 13" →

22"

Diagram A

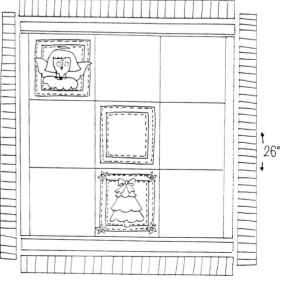

26"

Diagram B

Appliqués

1. Trace and cut Christmas shapes from Appliqué Patterns on page 126 as you desire, following General Appliqué Instructions on page 7.

2. Fuse shapes onto center of assembled 6½" blocks with fusible webbing as shown in Diagram B on page 90.

3. Using black permanent pen, pen-stitch around edges of shapes as you desire, following General Pen-stitching Instructions on page 9. Add details to appliqués as shown in photo on page 89. To add color, use a cotton swab to apply blush as you desire.

4. Outline and embellish appliqués as you desire. If using glitter glue, let blocks dry overnight before continuing.

Construction

1. With RST, sew 6½" blocks together as you desire as shown in Diagram B on page 90.

2. **1st Border:** With RST, sew 1¼" x 19" strips to top and bottom of quilt top. Trim off any excess fabric. With RST, sew 1¼" x 21" strips to sides of quilt top. Press seams toward border.

3. **Pieced Outside Border:** With RST, sew 2½" x 25½" pieced border to top and bottom of quilt top. Trim off any excess fabric. With RST, sew remaining pieced borders to sides of quilt top. Press seams towards border.

4. Finish quilt, following General Finishing Instructions on page 8.

Use the appliqués from this project to create these adorable Christmas bags, following instructions for Bloomin' Bunnies Gift Bags on pages 22–23. Send them home with goodies and stocking stuffers for young visitors.

Very Merry Christmas Socks

Cutting & Preparation

1. Cut 2 of Template 1 on page 95 from fabric, adding ¼" to all sides. Turn top edge of each sock under ½" and press.

2. Cut 1 of Template 1 from batting, adding ¼" to all sides. Cut ½" from top edge of batting sock.

3. Cut 1 each of Templates 2–6 on pages 95–96.

4. **Pieced Sock Cuff:** Cut (8) 1¼" x 3" strips and (7) 1½" x 3" strips. With RST, sew strips together alternating 1¼" strips with 1½" strips as shown in Diagram A.

5. Layer batting, front of sock, inner sock, heel, toe, and background together with right sides up as shown in Diagram B. Pin in place.

6. Sew around edge of inner sock, heel, toe, and background with a running stitch as shown in Diagram C, following General Embroidery Instructions on page 7.

These socks are simple, festive, and fast to make. Fill them with fabrics and notions for a fellow quilter or stuff them with toys and treats for your favorite kids. Whatever you do, don't forget to have fun!

Supplies Needed

Batting:
- 9" x 45"

Fabric:
- for appliqués, cuff, and loop, assorted scraps
- for inner sock, ¼ yard
- for sock, ⅓ yard

Notions:
- ¼ yard regular fusible webbing
- assorted buttons
- assorted colors embroidery floss
- fine-tip permanent black pen
- gold glitter glue (optional)

Diagram A

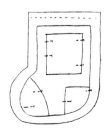

Diagram B

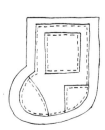

Diagram C

Appliqués

1. Trace and cut Christmas shapes from Appliqué Patterns on page 126 and several stars on page 118 as you desire, following General Appliqué Instructions on pages 6–7.
2. Fuse appliqués onto center of background with fusible webbing (shapes may overlap edges of square).
3. Sew buttons to center of each star. Using permanent pen, pen-stitch around edges of shapes as you desire, following General Pen-stitching Instructions on page 9. Add details to appliqués as shown in photo on page 92. To add color, use a cotton swab to apply blush as you desire.
4. Outline and embellish appliqués as you desire. If using glitter glue, let sock dry overnight before continuing.

Construction

1. With RST, sew assembled sock front to sock back, stopping and back-stitching at dot as shown in Diagram D. Clip seam to dot.
2. **Pieced Sock Strip:** With WST, press pieced strip in half lengthwise and finish raw edge with zigzag stitch as shown in Diagram E. Place finished raw edge of strip inside sock top, matching finished raw edge with edge of turned under seam allowance. Pin strip in place and topstitch to sock, trimming off any excess length as shown in Diagram F.
3. Turn sock wrong side out and pin unsewn section of sock together, matching pieced strip edges and sew. Turn right side out.
4. With RST, sew lengthwise seam of loop. Turn right side out. Fold loop in half and hand-stitch to inside of sock as shown in Diagram G.

Diagram D

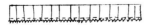

Diagram E

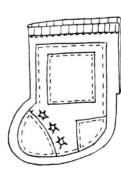

Diagram F

Diagram G

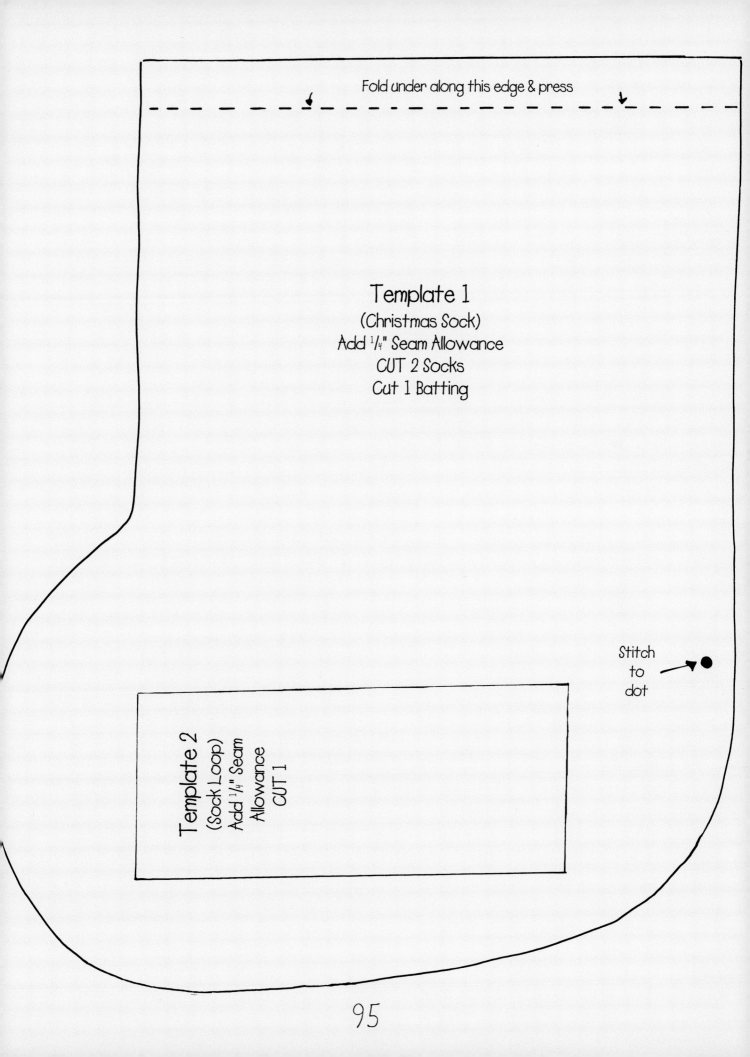

Fold under along this edge & press

Template 1
(Christmas Sock)
Add 1/4" Seam Allowance
CUT 2 Socks
Cut 1 Batting

Stitch
to
dot

Template 2
(Sock Loop)
Add 1/4" Seam Allowance
CUT 1

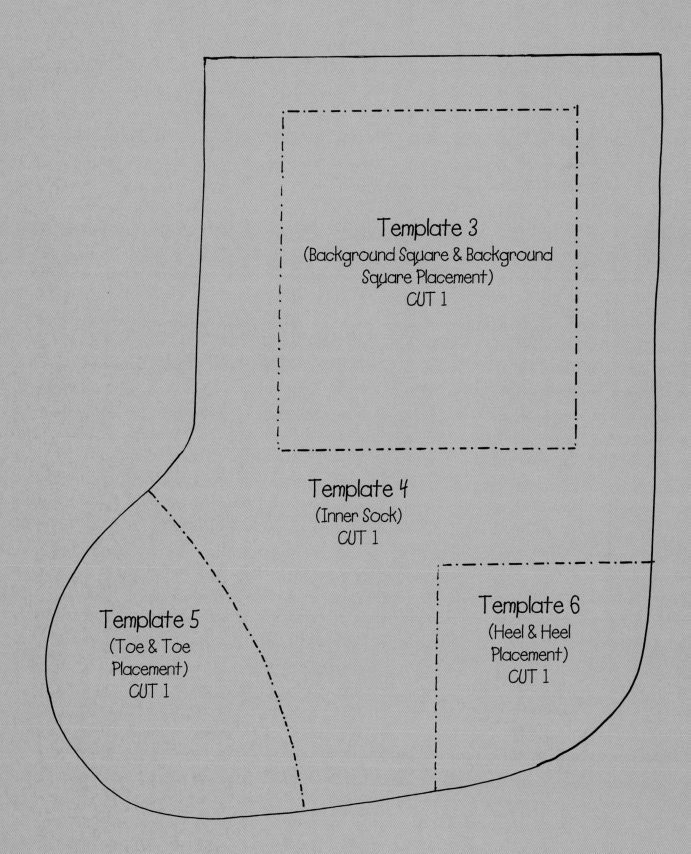

Template 3
(Background Square & Background
Square Placement)
CUT 1

Template 4
(Inner Sock)
CUT 1

Template 5
(Toe & Toe
Placement)
CUT 1

Template 6
(Heel & Heel
Placement)
CUT 1

Appliqué Patterns

Annie & Andy
Used with Annie & Andy Quilt,
Annie & Andy Pillow, Classic
Annie Jumper, and Classic
Andy Overalls.

Andy
Used with Annie & Andy Wall Pictures.

Enlarge 127%

Enlarge 127%

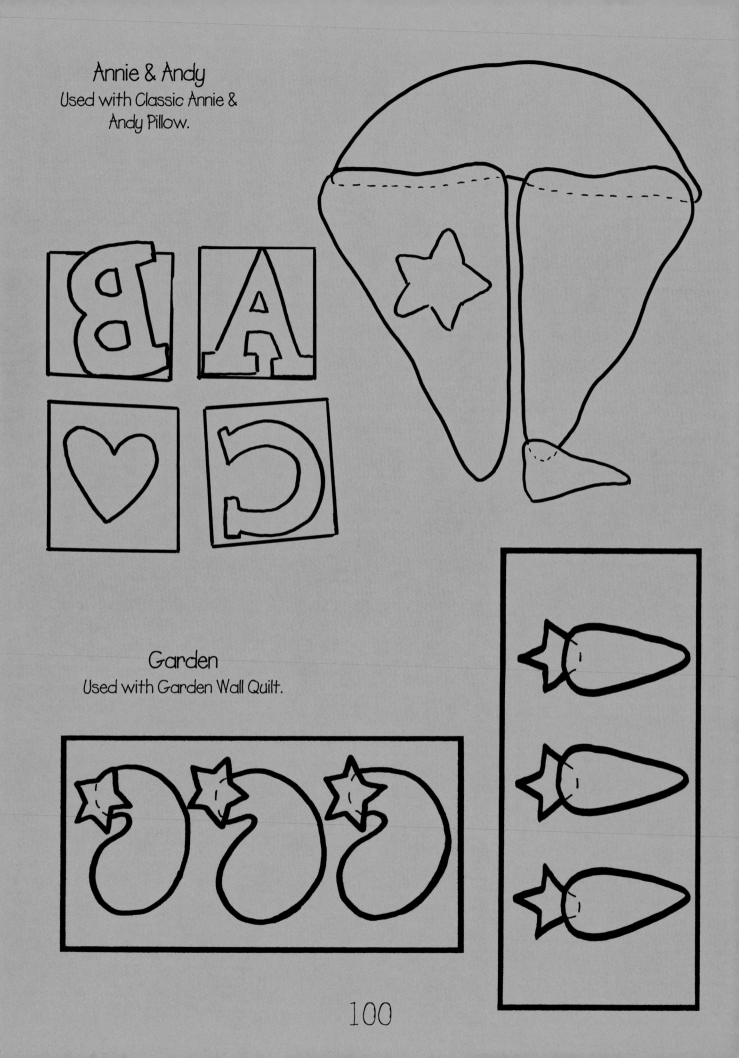

Annie & Andy
Used with Classic Annie &
Andy Pillow.

Garden
Used with Garden Wall Quilt.

100

Garden
Used with Garden
Wall Quilt.

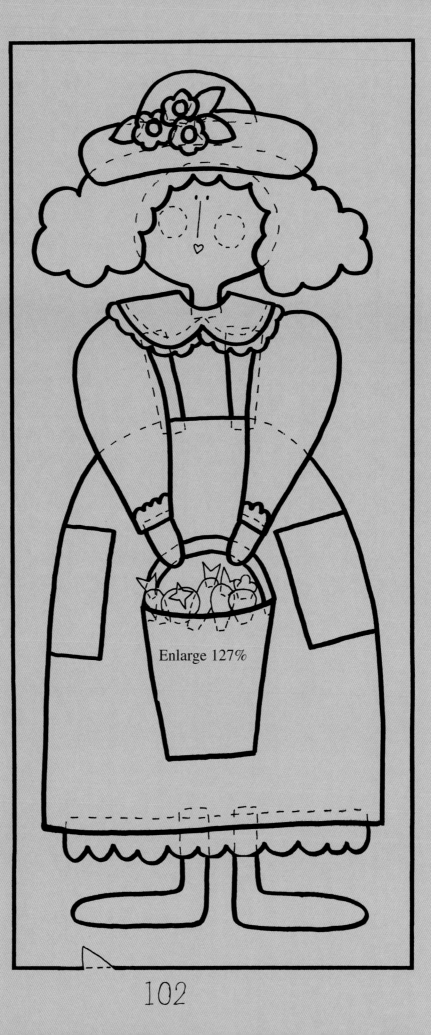

Enlarge 127%

Garden
Used with
Garden Wall
Quilt.

Garden
Used with Garden Wall Quilt.

Garden
Used with Garden Wall Quilt, Bloomin' Bunnies Gift Bags, and Bloomin' Bunnies Wall Quilt.

Garden
Used with Bloomin' Bunnies
Gift Bags and Bloomin'
Bunnies Wall Quilt.

Bunny
Used with Bloomin'
Bunnies Wall Quilt
and Bloomin' Bunnies
Wall Pictures.

Leaf

Leaf

108

Bunny
Used with Bloomin' Bunnies
Wall Quilt and Bloomin'
Bunnies Wall Pictures.

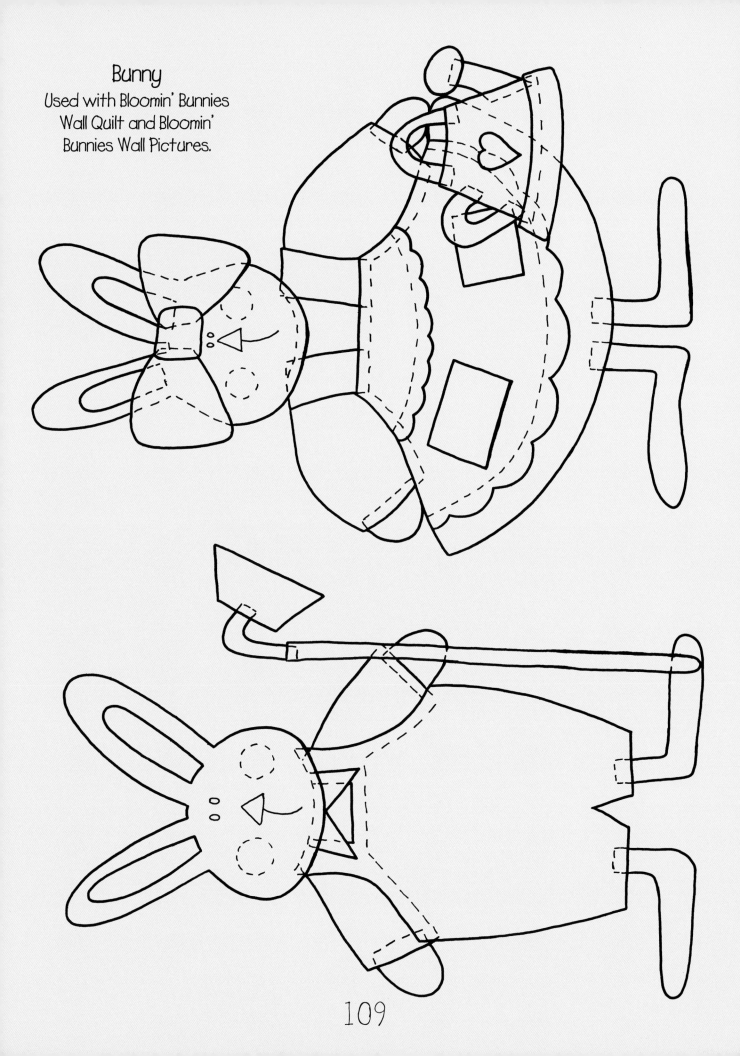

109

Bunny

Used with Bloomin' Bunnies
Wall Quilt and Bloomin'
Bunnies Wall Pictures.

110

Bunny
Used with Bloomin'
Bunnies Wall Quilt
and Bloomin'
Bunnies Wall
Pictures.

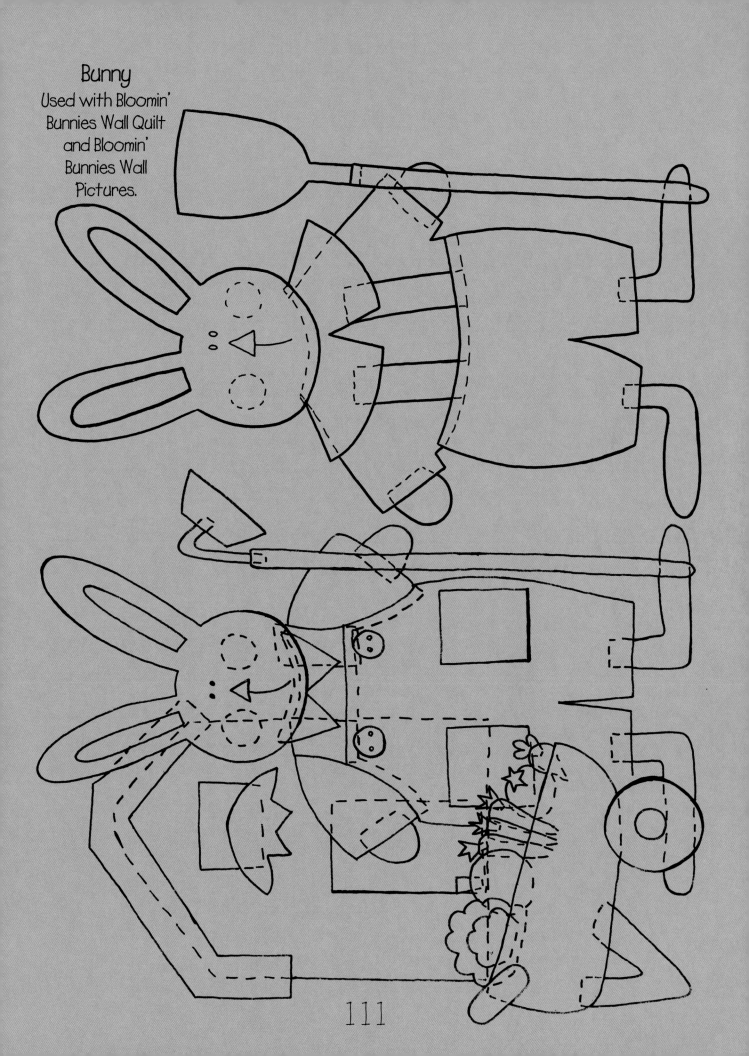

111

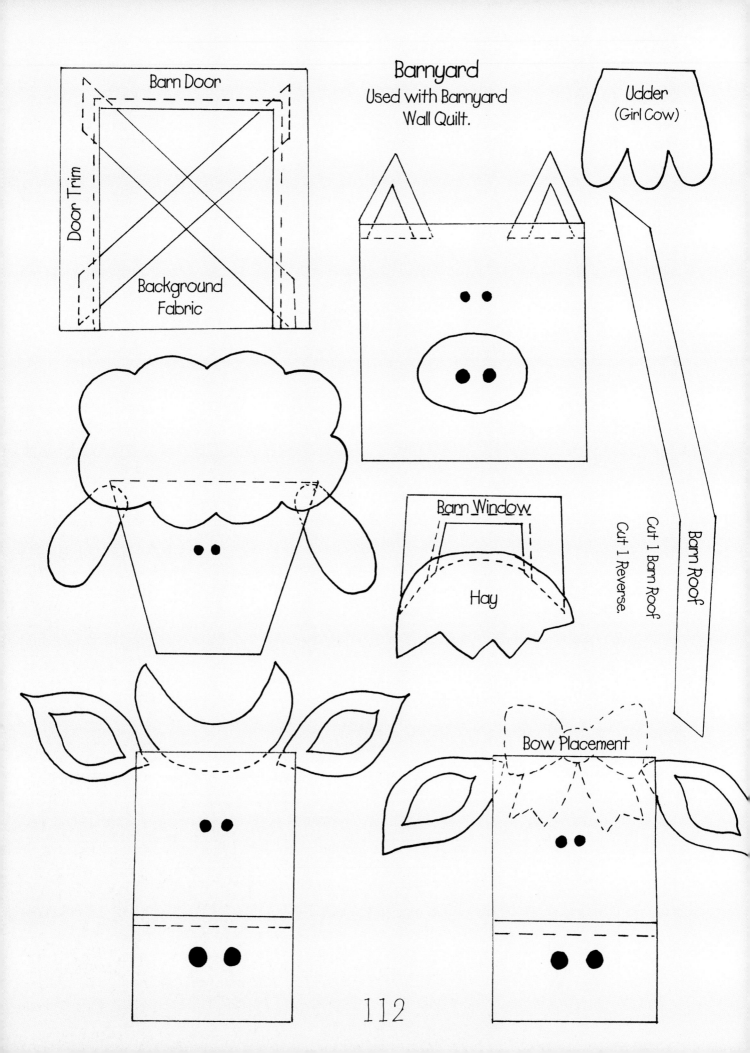

Barn Door

Door Trim

Background
Fabric

Barnyard
Used with Barnyard
Wall Quilt.

Udder
(Girl Cow)

Barn Window

Hay

Cut 1 Barn Roof

Cut 1 Reverse.

Barn Roof

Bow Placement

112

Bear
Used with
Baby Bear
Quilt.

113

Bug
Used with Fun & Friendly Bug Quilt and
Fun & Friendly Bug Pillow.

Dragonfly Wing
Cut 1 Dragonfly Wing.
Cut 1 Reverse.

Butterfly & Dragonfly Body

114

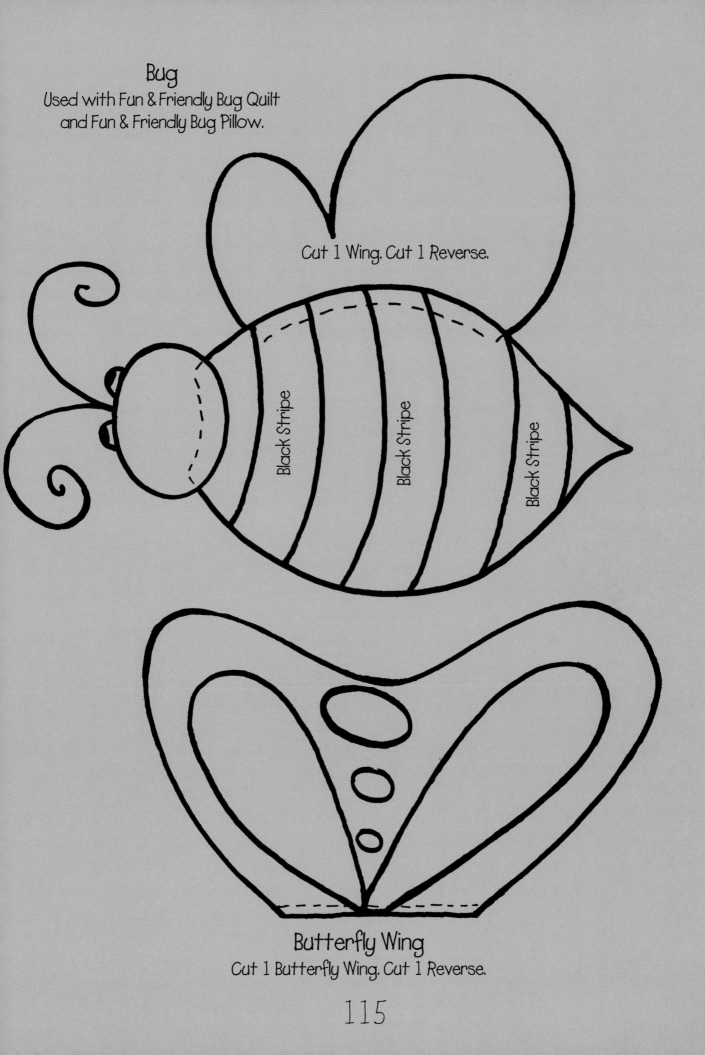

Bug
Used with Fun & Friendly Bug Quilt
and Fun & Friendly Bug Pillow.

Cut 1 Wing. Cut 1 Reverse.

Black Stripe

Black Stripe

Black Stripe

Butterfly Wing
Cut 1 Butterfly Wing. Cut 1 Reverse.

Bug
Used with Fun & Friendly Bug Quilt
and Fun & Friendly Bug Pillow.

Cut 1 Butterfly Wing. Cut 1 Reverse.

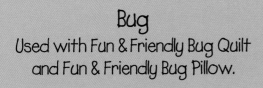

Bug
Used with Fun & Friendly Bug Quilt
and Fun & Friendly Bug Pillow.

Bug
Used with Fun & Friendly Bug Quilt
and Fun & Friendly Bug Pillow.

Garden Patch
Used with Annie & Andy Quilt
and Little Sprouts Baby
Vest.

Cut 1 Butterfly Wing. Cut 1 Reverse.

118

Garden Patch

Used with Garden Patch Jumpers and Loose Threads Patch Vest.

For girls' size 6

For girls' sizes 2-4

120

Garden Patch

Used with Garden Patch
Jumpers.

For girls' sizes 8-14

Garden Patch
Used with Garden Patch
Jumpers.

For women's sizes 6-14

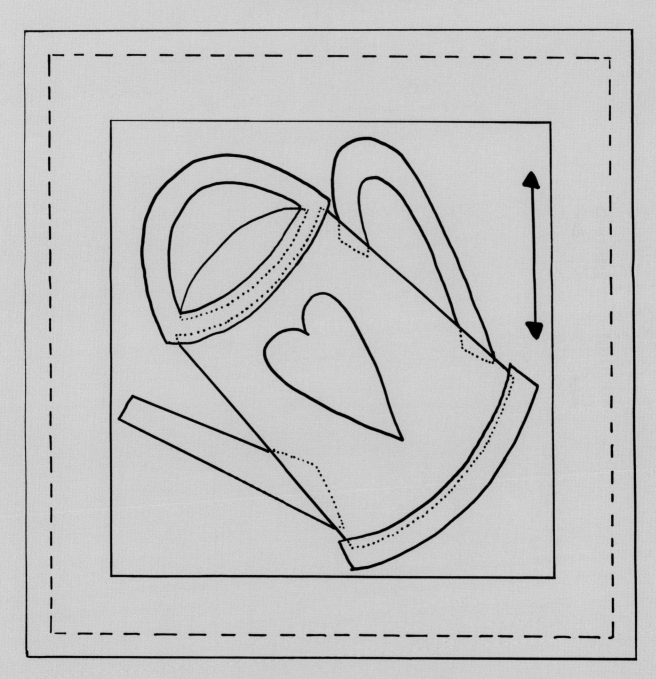

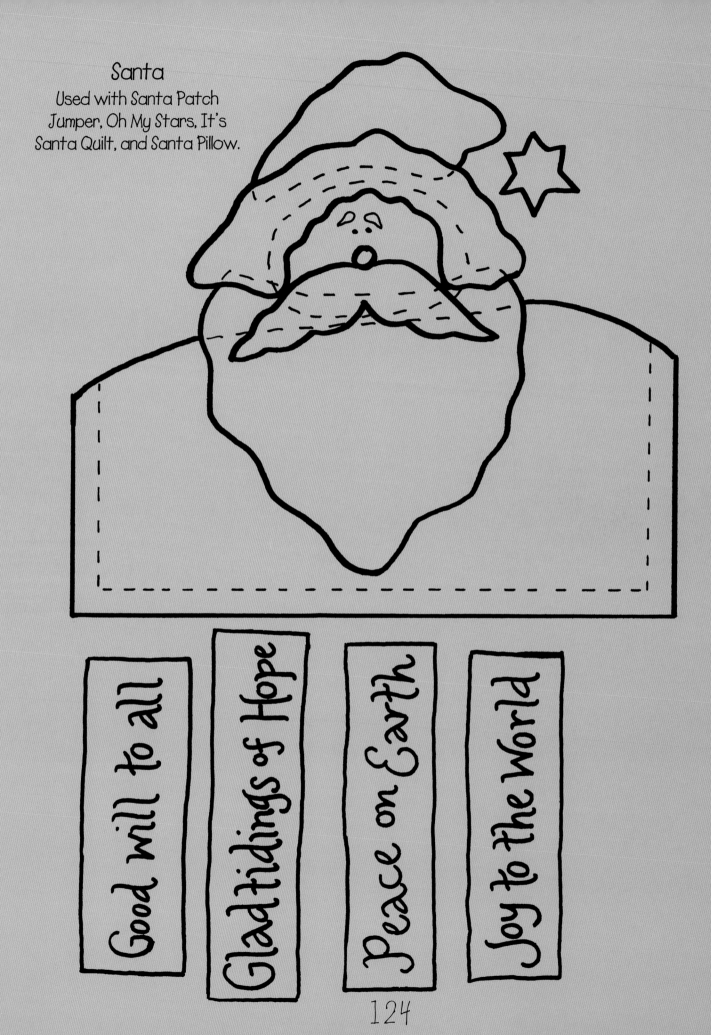

Santa
Used with Santa Patch
Jumper, Oh My Stars, It's
Santa Quilt, and Santa Pillow.

Good will to all

Glad tidings of Hope

Peace on Earth

Joy to the World

Santa
Used with Santa Pillow.

Christmas
Used with Very Merry
Christmas Socks and Very
Merry Christmas Wall Quilt.

Enlarge 25%

Enlarge 25%

Enlarge 25%

Enlarge 25%

Enlarge 25%

1st Layer of Poinsettia

Enlarge 25%

Enlarge 25%

Enlarge 25%

Enlarge 25%

Enlarge 25%

Enlarge 25%

2nd Layer of Poinsettia

126

Metric Conversion Charts

	cm—Centimetres Inches to Centimetres								
inches	cm	inches	cm	inches	cm	inches	cm	inches	cm
⅛	0.3	3	7.6	13	33.0	25	63.5	38	96.5
¼	0.6	3½	8.9	14	35.6	26	66.0	39	99.1
½	1.3	4	10.2	15	38.1	27	68.6	40	101.6
⅝	1.6	4½	11.4	16	40.6	28	71.1	41	104.1
¾	1.9	5	12.7	17	43.2	29	73.7	42	106.7
⅞	2.2	6	15.2	18	45.7	30	76.2	43	109.2
1	2.5	7	17.8	19	48.3	31	78.7	44	111.8
1¼	3.2	8	20.3	20	50.8	33	83.8	45	114.3
1½	3.8	9	22.9	21	53.3	34	86.4	46	116.8
1¾	4.4	10	25.4	22	55.9	35	88.9	47	119.4
2	5.1	11	27.9	23	58.4	36	91.4	48	121.9
2½	6.4	12	30.5	24	61.0	37	94.0	49	124.5

Yards to Metres									
Yards	Metres	Yards	Metres	Yards	Metres	Yards	Metres	Yards	Metres
⅛	0.11	2⅛	1.94	4⅛	3.77	6⅛	5.60	8⅛	7.43
¼	0.23	2¼	2.06	4¼	3.89	6¼	5.72	8¼	7.54
⅜	0.34	2⅜	2.17	4⅜	4.00	6⅜	5.83	8⅜	7.66
½	0.46	2½	2.29	4½	4.11	6½	5.94	8½	7.77
⅝	0.57	2⅝	2.40	4⅝	4.23	6⅝	6.06	8⅝	7.89
¾	0.69	2¾	2.51	4¾	4.34	6¾	6.17	8¾	8.00
⅞	0.80	2⅞	2.63	4⅞	4.46	6⅞	6.29	8⅞	8.12
1	0.91	3	2.74	5	4.57	7	6.40	9	8.23
1⅛	1.03	3⅛	2.86	5⅛	4.69	7⅛	6.52	9⅛	8.34
1¼	1.14	3¼	2.97	5¼	4.80	7¼	6.63	9¼	8.46
1⅜	1.26	3⅜	3.09	5⅜	4.91	7⅜	6.74	9⅜	8.57
1½	1.37	3½	3.20	5½	5.03	7½	6.86	9½	8.69
1⅝	1.49	3⅝	3.31	5⅝	5.14	7⅝	6.97	9⅝	8.80
1¾	1.60	3¾	3.43	5¾	5.26	7¾	7.09	9¾	8.92
1⅞	1.71	3⅞	3.54	5⅞	5.37	7⅞	7.20	9⅞	9.03
2	1.83	4	3.66	6	5.49	8	7.32	10	9.14

Index